H̲E̲A̲L̲
with
FOODS

Manjari Chandra is a functional nutritionist, wellness coach and author of *Eat Up, Clean Up*. She is also the founder of Manjari Wellness—a platform providing holistic consultation to help people lead a healthy lifestyle with proper nutrition.

She works as a consultant functional nutritionist at Daivam and has been offering her services in leading hospitals of India, including Max Healthcare, Manipal Hospital, Columbia Asia and many more. Having more than 20 years of work experience, she has been at the forefront advocating changes in lifestyle and consumption of nutritious food. Her contributions to the field have helped her win the Global Choice Award 2021, 'Women Icon of the Year (Wellness Author and Coach)', ASSOCHAM Award for 'Popular Consultant in the Field of Wellness and Nutrition' and many others.

Manjari has also appeared as a health expert on multiple television channels, including NDTV, India Today, Zee Business, Mirror Now and Aaj Tak. She lives in New Delhi with her husband and two daughters.

Praise for the Book

A must-read book that simplifies how food affects us and how we can make the right choices, not only in terms of ingredients but also in how we consume them. Very valuable in today's world where information and options can be overwhelming.

—Sonali Bendre Behl
Bollywood actress

Exercising, along with eating right, can work wonders for your fitness. This book tells you how your kitchen can be your own clinic. Our Indian kitchens have all the ingredients needed for staying healthy and happy. Read the book to know about it.

—Major D.P. Singh
Kargil war veteran, India's first blade runner, national award winner, named in Asia Book of Records for being the first solo skydiver with disabilities and in Limca Book of Records' 'People of the Year, 2016' list

Reading this book may be your first step towards healthier living. Manjari does an excellent job of guiding you through what's most important for you, the reader, right now. Take this first step and you will be forever grateful for the journey you have undertaken.

—Dr Tom O'Bryan
Celebrated author, expert in functional medicine and autoimmune disease, founder of Dr.com, faculty at Institute of Functional Medicine, chief health officer at KnoWEwell

HEAL
with
FOODS

MAGICAL INGREDIENTS
THAT WILL CHANGE YOUR LIFE

MANJARI CHANDRA

RUPA

Published by
Rupa Publications India Pvt. Ltd 2022
7/16, Ansari Road, Daryaganj
New Delhi 110002

Sales Centres:
Allahabad Bengaluru Chennai
Hyderabad Jaipur Kathmandu
Kolkata Mumbai

ISBN: 978-93-5520-093-8

Third impression 2022

10 9 8 7 6 5 4 3

The moral right of the author has been asserted.

Printed in India

For my mother, who shaped me into who I am today and remained the driving force behind my success. She nurtured everyone with great panache and motherly love—her anecdotes will continue to frame our stories.

And for my father, who survived her and has always been a strong pillar throughout my life.

And to my incredibly supportive husband and two lovely daughters, I am grateful for the encouragement and inspiration you continue to instill in me.

CONTENTS

FOREWORD

A healthy diet, along with physical activity, is fundamental element of health and wellness. But, with no time to take care of one's health and readily available unhealthy temptations around, having a balanced diet is easier said than achieved. Moreover, there are still many misconceptions around healthy foods, with everybody becoming a nutrition expert nowadays.

More than what to eat, when to eat and how much to eat are important aspects of healthy eating. With misleading information available on healthy foods and their preparations, the need for a credible source goes up.

Heal with Foods is one such book that is backed by in-depth research and is full of useful information about foods that have the potential to heal. Being someone who has advocated for beauty through natural ways, I find this book both effective and relevant in today's time.

From addressing issues like reasons for unhealthy food choices and importance of gut health to re-discovering those magical forgotten foods, Manjari has tried to add every possible ingredient of health and wellness in the book.

I can associate myself with Manjari's idea of nutrition that has its roots in nature. I particularly like her idea of shifting to traditional ways of cooking and eating. Beauty, according to me, is a reflection of one's health and wellness. And when you eat right, choosing natural and seasonal foods, you will be healthy from inside and beautiful from outside.

I am quite impressed by Manjari's work in the field of health and nutrition and this book is one such sincere effort to help people regain health and wellness, increasing their reliability on food than medicines.

Now, I leave you readers with the book. Have a happy read.

Dr Blossom Kochhar
Chairperson of Blossom
Kochhar Group of Companies

INTRODUCTION

Amidst all the information available through different media channels, *Heal with Foods* attempts to simplify healing and being healthy by focusing on what we eat. It takes the reader on a journey to rediscover nutritious foods items which were once highly regarded by the previous generations but came to be overshadowed and forgotten as the food industry grew.

The book serves as a mirror to reflect our current eating behaviour, explaining how we have reached here by revealing the factors that influence our food choices. Later, it highlights life-changing ingredients that can serve as a magical remedy to not only prevent but also reverse the progression of various chronic disorders. It shares nutritional insights of these magical ingredients that can contribute to enhancing personal well-being.

The gut defines and influences every aspect of our health, from digestion, body weight, mood to hormonal balance and immunity. As the gut begins to heal, our body eventually detoxifies itself; the gut health can only be enhanced by eating nutritional food. Offering metabolic insights, the book emphasizes on promoting gut health and explains how the intestine impacts our overall well-being.

With the pandemic, maintaining one's health has become a priority for everybody. Taking undue advantage, food companies are misleading consumers with claims about the health benefits their products offer. The book steps in here focusing on providing natural, wholesome alternatives to our current unhealthy eating habits. It provides simple yet powerful options which have been overlooked over the years but contain magical properties to improve our health.

Serving its main purpose, the book provides practical solutions presenting recipes prepared with readily available natural food items. It empowers the reader to use natural foods, herbs and spices to prepare their main meals, salads, side-dishes, pickles, smoothies, etc. The reader will be in for a surprise when they realize how easily available and cheap these food items are. Once the book sows the seed of knowledge about these, you will consciously look for the same when you go to the market next time.

The inspiration for the book came from daily interactions with my patients and family members, and I realized that people are not actively looking for healthier options to eat. They start showing resentment towards making traditional recipes from foods they consume daily. People are not aware of how nutritionally rich ingredients, herbs and spices can be used to add flavour to their otherwise bland meals. Further, they are caught up in a vicious circle of work and a flamboyant lifestyle, not allowing them to spend extra time in the kitchen preparing fresh food.

The book is for anyone open to exploring beyond a few popular food options. My experience as a wife, mother and functional nutritionist prompted me to share about the effects of food on our health. But addressing and acknowledging the issue is only halfway forward to solving the problem. One must discuss feasible solutions applicable for everyone. This is where the book takes a giant leap and stands out from other works in the market.

Takeaway for the Readers

Eating industrially-processed food items and those high in sugar cause inflammation in our body, which impacts our immunity, deteriorates our health and leads to chronic disorders. On the contrary, healthy eating habits simply involve eating natural, wholesome and home-cooked food. Buying fresh vegetables from the market and giving an hour of our day to prepare nutritious meals goes a long way in getting rid of inflammation. The book shows how conveniently it can be done.

The book is intended for the awareness and education of a general audience. Every attempt has been made to ensure that all information compiled is from validated research and credible sources. The book has been strategically divided into three major parts.

The first part offers insights into our current food preferences and forces the reader to reflect upon the factors prompting us to eat unhealthy food. Further, it discusses the detrimental impact of our current food choices on our physical, emotional and mental health.

The second part puts forward a question as to how we can rejuvenate our gut microbiome, which comprises the bacteria living in the lower part of the intestine affecting our health. The book then provides the reader with two words as an answer—prebiotics and probiotics. This segment of the book describes the direct positive effects of prebiotics and probiotics on our gut, which in turn is responsible for boosting immunity, developing cognition, promoting cardiometabolic health, improving digestive health and maintaining mental well-being.

xiv • HEAL WITH FOODS

Life-Changing Magical Ingredients

The third and the most important part of the book presents a broad range of 'magical' ingredients offering invaluable health benefits. We often overlook these ingredients in the supermarket. The primary focus of this segment is to present healthier food choices that come not only packed with nutrition but also soothing and pleasing taste for the palate. These ingredients are readily available at a reasonable price; the best part is that they can be as conveniently cooked or consumed as any other vegetable or fruit.

This part of the book talks about various green leafy vegetables, fruits and millets that provide all the good fat, protein and complex carbohydrates one essentially needs. Some herbs, spices, nuts and seeds added to this will fulfill one's daily micronutrient requirements.

Each chapter summarizes the nutritional profile and benefits of various food items while presenting lip-smacking and easy-to-prepare recipes. Since not all the recipes could be mentioned here, we have outlined the simplest ones to help the readers incorporate the ingredients in their daily diet. The book will make you rethink about the food items you buy in the market and provide you with healthier options to explore. It allows you to gain a fresh perspective on nutrition as a core facet of healing and being healthy. The book intends to restore faith in the naturally available foods to receive a balanced nutritious diet. It will empower the readers to prepare healthy snacks, side dishes and meals at home without sweating out tirelessly in the kitchen for hours.

Part I

_____

OUR FOOD CHOICES

1

WHO MAKES OUR FOOD CHOICES?

It's a Friday morning and a typical day for Sabrina—a homemaker in her late 30s, mother of two and a caring wife. She finishes her early morning household chores that include sending kids to school, preparing breakfast for everybody and ensuring her mother-in-law gets her tea on time.

Additionally, she has to make sure that all the utensils are kept in the washing sink and all the relevant places are dusted before the maid comes in at 9.30 a.m. Once the maid is gone, she takes a breather and then gets ready to go to the supermarket to get some groceries.

As she is preparing to leave, she meets her tenant, Rabhya, at the gate. Rabhya is pursuing graduation from a nearby college and lives with her friend in a rented accommodation. She took an off from college to study for her upcoming exams. As they exchange greetings, Rabhya tells Sabrina that she too is heading to the supermarket to buy food for the weekend and offers her a ride on her scooty.

Sabrina barely gets time to meet her friends. She finds this chance as a perfect opportunity to call her best friend, Shruti, who got married recently and happens to live nearby. Shruti, who was planning to go buy some cosmetics, agrees to meet her.

After a few minutes of chattering in the supermarket,

the three grab hold of their trolleys and start exploring the counters.

Rabhya, being impulsive, picks up whatever meets her eyes. She pulls many items from the first two shelves of the food aisle. These include multiple packets of potato chips, fruit cake, instant noodles, aerated drinks, coffee, eggs and milk. Additionally, she buys some chocolates thinking that they are beneficial in reducing stress and anxiety.

'Look at you girl, already done with it,' exclaims Sabrina looking at how quickly Rabhya has finished her shopping. She asks, 'Aren't you going to buy anything else?'

Rabhya replies, 'No! Here's everything we need to munch on for the weekend. These are either easy-to-prepare or ready-to-eat. Mostly, we need these during breakfast or for nights when we watch movies or study till late. Otherwise, we have our lunch at the college canteen and dinner comes from the Punjabi restaurant.'

Sabrina, on the other hand, has her task cut out. She has to buy the weekly ration; it does not include a heavyweight bag of rice or flour, but other small yet critical ingredients and food items that are consumed on a daily basis.

First, she picks a few packs of salted snacks (namkeens), juice boxes, tea, coffee and sugar. She desires to buy whole almonds and pistachios but decides against it after seeing their price. Instead, she buys a couple of packs of salted peanuts.

While moving forward, she accidentally glances upon a new brand of refined oil. She remembers its advertisement on TV claiming to be cholesterol-free and having omega-3 which is good for the heart. She immediately pulls a two-litre plastic can of the oil and does not even bother looking at the rest of its content or the other types of cooking oil kept there.

Next, she picks up gram flour (besan) with the thought of

preparing frying fitters—as her kids love them—using the new oil. Then she goes to the vegetables and fruits section. Given that she does not have to walk back on foot but has a ride, Sabrina buys 3–4 kg each of potatoes and onions to be used for preparing fritters the subsequent day and aloo paronthe on Sunday. She also buys cabbage and beans. Additionally, she buys a kilogram each of apples, mangoes and bananas because everybody at home loves those.

As she is exploring other options, she thinks of preparing a traditional dessert that night—kheer (a form of rice pudding). This dessert requires rice, milk, sugar and some cardamom for flavouring as its core ingredients. So, she buys half a kg of extra rice, sugar and milk along with a small packet of cardamom. Keeping in mind that her husband is fond of non-vegetarian food, she buys some frozen chicken, which she plans to serve after deep-frying.

As she is picking up a couple of packets of frozen chicken from the refrigerator, Shruti enters the food section after shopping for cosmetics. She calls for Sabrina who is standing at a distance, 'Hey! Is there any stuff for vegetarians like us?'

Sabrina smiles, 'Yes, yes! Here are some frozen cheese nuggets and potato tikki kept in the other refrigerator. Come, grab some!'

Shruti not only grabs a few packets of frozen food but also pulls a couple of large bottles of aerated soft drinks. 'You know, there's a cricket match this Sunday and my husband is inviting his friends to come over and watch it together. So...'

Sabrina replies all too knowingly, 'Yeah, I can understand. We too host numerous guests regularly. Sometimes I think I should turn my house into a motel and demand payment from them on a per hour basis (both of them chuckle). You see this entire stack of packets of namkeens and cookies are for unknown guests who are going to visit this weekend and then the coming week.'

As they are walking to the payment counter, Sabrina notices that Shruti is constantly surfing something on the internet in her phone. She curiously asks, 'What is it you're looking for in your phone? I have been noticing you for quite some time now. A few more minutes on and I think you will teleport inside the phone.'

Shruti laughs and tells her, 'See, today is Friday. Tomorrow is off. So I asked my husband if we could go out for a romantic dinner. He agreed to it and asked me to look for a fancy restaurant. Just the other day, I saw a recommendation by a food blogger about this Italian restaurant, and I have forgotten its name. They have amazing varieties of crispy starters and their dessert, tiramisu, is delicious! I have never been to that place, and today I would love to.' Still lost in the phone, she continues, 'Even my friend, hailing from a high-end social circle, went there last week with her boyfriend.'

And suddenly, it strikes her that she should check out her friend's Facebook posts for some information. She opens the profile and within a few seconds comes across her recent check-in at the same Italian restaurant she was talking about. She jumps with joy, 'Got it! Got it! I got it!' She immediately opens the online booking app and reserves a table for two for the night.

Rabhya, by that moment, has already got her billing done and is waiting for Sabrina and Shruti. As they both make their payments, Sabrina wishes Shruti a wonderful time in the evening.

Rabhya, looking astounded by how many things Sabrina bought, said, 'I would have brought my SUV had I known you were going to buy this much.' Both laugh. They take five more minutes to keep all the groceries inside the scooty before riding away.

◆

REFLECTING UPON OUR FOOD PREFERENCES

What do we get to learn about our general food preferences after reading the above scenario? What do we realize regarding our behaviour as a customer when it comes to food? Overall, it looks unhealthy, right? If you find a couple of similarities between the above example and the way you or your kids buy groceries, then that's a problem to be acknowledged. And if you recognize a remarkable resemblance, then that's a matter of concern which requires to be dealt with diligently.

Therefore, before we even begin discussing life-changing diet and magical ingredients offering health benefits, we must reflect upon:

- Where are we going wrong and why?
- What factors are driving us to buy unhealthy food items and indulge in bad eating habits?
- How do our current food choices impact our physical, emotional and mental health?

We will discuss the first two points in this chapter and deal with the third in the next.

If It's in Your Mind, It's in Your Stomach

Mostly, what we buy and eat is the result of what we see. There is a persistent strategy by food companies to display their products repeatedly through advertisements. This is done so subtly and steadily that our consciousness does not get bothered by it. Rather, receiving information about a specific product becomes part of our routine.

Consider how Sabrina bought the refined oil. Most probably, she had enough cooking oil at her home, but when she glanced at the oil can, she recognized the brand from the TV commercial that she had come across every now and then.

She must have seen the advertisement more than 20 times a day, often not even realizing that she was watching it. When she comes across the same oil can in the supermarket, her subconscious mind relays all the information to her regarding the features she liked. With that information, she decided to buy the new cooking oil.

Meanwhile, Rabhya's decision is influenced by her need to save on time as she has to study, get enough sleep and also enjoy TV series and movies. This leaves her no time to cook fresh food; her choices trickle down to ordering from a restaurant or preparing some instant recipe with eggs and/or noodles. As for Shruti, she is influenced by contemporary social media trends. She makes a decision on the basis of what her friends are doing and recommending.

We do not buy or eat what we actually need. We buy what we see the most, hear about the most and what's available easily. This habit is perpetuated by what's being constantly thrown at us in the form of advertisements, hoardings and social media posts.

And generally, what's available most easily? Fast food, junk food, sweets, aerated soft drinks and fried food. The market is flooded with 'healthy' labelled food products packed with artificial goodness. We do not tend to explore beyond what's displayed in front of us.

How Many of You Look at the Second Page of a Google Search?

The same question is applicable when we talk about exploring healthier food options at a supermarket. There's always a lot more to it than meets the eye. Our eating habits are more centred on satiating hunger and not necessarily on getting enough nutrition. So, let's try to understand the underlying factors that are luring us into buying and eating certain foods that we think we need, but actually don't. These factors might not seem obvious to us because they are built up very subtly but have the power to influence our decision-making.

FACTORS AFFECTING CONTEMPORARY CONSUMER BEHAVIOUR AND FOOD PREFERENCES

These factors include, but are not limited to, the following:

1. Vibrant advertisements

A single advertisement when shown over and over again imbeds in our subconscious mind creating an inclination towards that product. When we find that same product in market, our subconscious mind transfers the information to our consciousness, making us buy that product almost impulsively.

Food companies try to attach an emotional aspect to their product so that a consumer can be more receptive. We all remember the commercial of Dhara cooking oil in the mid-90s. An upset kid exclaiming with joy, 'Jalebi!' is etched in our memories.

Though it is good advertising touching the raw emotions of consumers, it does not necessarily mean that the product is healthy. Advertisements about refined oil will boast about the taste of the food cooked using that oil. They will claim that it has zero cholesterol. The truth is that refined oils are plant-based products that anyway do not have cholesterol. Instead, they have significant levels of triglycerides which pose excessive threat to our cardiovascular system. Elevated triglyceride levels have been clinically shown to increase the risk of cardiovascular diseases.

An advertisement of a chocolate associates the product with love and friendship, but it never mentions the inflammatory effects of the sugar present in the product. Soda advertisements boast about refreshment, but they do not want you to know that it contains 6 tablespoons of sugar per 100 ml. The only reason you do not vomit after gulping down soft drinks is because of the presence of phosphoric acid in it. Celebrities, despite endorsing them, will never personally consume those products.

Recent studies have proved that advertisements for foods and beverages have a more adverse effect on children and teenagers.[1] [2] Additionally, parental control does not have any substantial or sustainable impact. Lucrative offers like 'buy one, get one' and bigger packets lure customers into buying more of these products.

Brands of food and beverage companies try to lure customers by attaching their fantasies and desires to their products. For example, soda advertisements typically show a

[1] Mary Story and Simone French, 'Food Advertising and Marketing Directed at Children and Adolescents in the US', *International Journal of Behavioural Nutrition and Physical Activity*, 2004.

[2] Adena Pinto, Elise Pauzé, Rachel Mutata, Marie-Hélène Roy-Gagnon, and Monique Potvin Kent, 'Food and Beverage Advertising to Children and Adolescents on Television: A Baseline Study', *International Journal of Environmental Research and Public Health*, 1999.

fit, stylish guy to whom a young woman gets easily attracted to. Juice advertisements will try convincing that children become sharper and more active after consuming their product citing it has loads of vitamins. And companies making cereal-based products will mislead you to believe that their product is the healthiest with added oats.

Oats or vitamins are undoubtedly good for health. However, there is no way of proving whether these so-called 'healthy' food products are boosting our immunity or helping us stay fit for the same have added emulsifiers, preservatives, sugar and other inflammatory ingredients which tend to go unnoticed by consumers.

2. Social trends and peer influence:
What's my friend having?

We have an inherent desire to gel with a group of batchmates or colleagues. To feel accepted and valued by friends, we exhibit certain types of behaviours that we otherwise wouldn't. We also model this behaviour in making our food preferences, especially when we have to decide on what to eat or drink with our friends. There are people who end up drinking alcohol because they have friends who do. This is an example of succumbing to peer influence. At times, they choose to drink only to avoid being left out.

There are some who simply call themselves social drinkers because they do not like drinking alone and prefer drinking at social gatherings and parties. Despite knowing that drinking is detrimental for health, we build up situations which give us an excuse to drink together.

Further, people like to follow the latest trends and visit places that come highly recommended by their friends. Things are no different when it comes to trying out new cafes and restaurants. People using social media platforms pay attention to what their friends are eating and where they are going for dinner. We seem to be accounting for others' lifestyles while forming personal eating habits.

So, if we notice our friends eating plenty of fruits and vegetables, we're more likely to consume the same. Likewise, if we observe our friends gorging on a lot of snacks and sugary drinks, we too tend to become careless about eating the right kind of food. As a result, we happen to follow their suit.

Similarly, when we see our peers going to high-end restaurants trying out international cuisines, it drives us to hang out at a similar place with our partners. Dining at a fancy restaurant brings out a sense of affluence and satisfies our desire to live a quality life. An urge to drink with friends or in parties also stems from the same motive.

Revisiting Shruti's desire to dine at an Italian restaurant with her husband, we can say one thing for sure: Italian cuisine is one of the best in serving richly flavoured foods with a lot of variety. Indians, especially, are obsessed with Chinese and Italian cuisines. People are lured watching their friends go out to lavish restaurants, shredding off their desi avatar and blending in with the modern style of living. So, the obsession of leading a specific lifestyle forces people to change their eating habits which, unfortunately, shift towards an unhealthy spectrum in most cases.

All the items that Shruti wished to taste—pizza, pasta lasagna and tiramisu—have high carbohydrate content with refined sugars and almost zero dietary fibre.

On the other hand, dieticians all over the world are recommending their clients to avoid white-coloured foods. It is because they are either polished or refined, containing high contents of starch and simple carbohydrates. Rice, table sugar, pizza, pasta and sandwich bread are examples of such kinds of foods.

Now, if you compare this list of food with what Shruti is most likely to eat, it is clear that she would have at least four out of the five white-coloured foods mentioned above in one form or the other. Well, this is not the worst part; the real problem will arise when it will become a routine. She will be tempted to eat such food every time she would go out for dinner, attend a party or order from a restaurant.

People tend to opt for food that is heavy on stomach and the most flavourful. And this is true with all cuisines, be it Italian, Mexican, Chinese or Indian. We do not realize that what seems delicious is, in effect, causing harm to our body when consumed regularly.

FOOD FOR THOUGHT

- Considering the arbitrary names of two different restaurants serving different cuisines, which would you rather choose to post a check-in about on Facebook—Desi Dhaba or Café Esposito?
- Which meal will you choose for posting its picture as your Instagram or WhatsApp story? Will it be *Sarso da Saag* with *chaas (buttermilk)* or lasgagna, pasta with a truffle pastry?

3. Well, not so well-informed!

Fruits are considered healthy. When we visit a sick person, we customarily take fruits for them as a kind gesture. We consider fruit juices to be healthy, which indeed they are, but not when industrially processed and sold in packed boxes that we buy from grocery stores. The presence of additives, preservatives, emulsifiers, along with added sugar, make these fruit-based products unfit to be consumed.

Facts Concerning High-Carbohydrate Diet vs High-Fat Diet

i. **Carbohydrate metabolizes into fat:** Dietary carbohydrate breaks down into glucose upon digestion. And as it happens, the pancreas releases insulin, which signals the cells to convert that glucose into energy. Insulin is also a fat-storing hormone, which facilitates the storage of fat either in the liver or in the form of adipose tissue (commonly known as body fat) under the skin and around internal organs.

ii. **Fat does not metabolize into fat:** On the contrary, fat intake does not evoke insulin response from the pancreas, avoiding fat storage inside the body. The consumed fat is then used for energy generation, synthesis of hormones and neurotransmitters and much more. Even extra fat consumed does not get stored as fat but is gradually converted into energy (two times more than that from glucose) in a sustainable manner throughout the day.

The 'Healthy' Claims Are Not So Healthy

Companies making refined oil sell their product indicating that it has omega-3[3] and is cholesterol-free. But what they do not describe is how insufficient the actual amount of omega-3 is in the product. Cabbage, cauliflower or broccoli can provide way more omega-3 than a litre of any refined oil can.

---

[3]Healthy fatty acid known for reducing the risk of cardiovascular disorders.

Additionally, most of these chemically processed cooking oils contain trans fat, which is an inflammatory component contributing to chronic illnesses like obesity, diabetes and cardiovascular disorders. Furthermore, these oils comprise triglycerides that increase the risk of a heart attack.

Companies making chips boast about having no trans fat in their products, but they contain a high concentration of sodium which increases the blood pressure. And when these products are consumed regularly, they increase the risk of not only hypertension but also stroke, heart failure and stomach cancer.

Consuming whole grains is better than eating refined flour, the reasons for which shall be explained later in the book. A product labelled as 'multigrain' implies that it contains more than one type of grain; however, it does not necessarily mean that the product has grains in the whole form. More importantly, these different grains like oats, millets and barley are present only in traces. Primary grain, wheat, remains in its typical refined form. Therefore, you must always check the ingredient list for words like 'whole' before the name of the cereal, for example, whole wheat. And also, review the actual amount of any grain present in per 100 g of the product.

Lastly, the products labelled as 'sugar-free' contain artificial sweeteners. These sweeteners evoke a similar, or at times even worse, insulin response as compared to natural sugar. Hence, they do not provide respite in controlling blood sugar levels. Instead, studies show that these sweeteners are potentially carcinogenic, increasing the risk of cancer.[4] [5] Additionally,

[4]Philip J. Landrigan and Kurt Straif, 'Aspartame and cancer—new evidence for causation', *Environmental Health*, 2021.

[5]James Huff and Joseph LaDou, 'Aspartame bioassay findings portend human

they are neurotoxic in nature and cause chronic inflammation when consumed regularly. So, think again before buying a diet beverage, artificially sweetened cookies or sugar-free sweeteners to add in your coffee or tea.

The 'Fine' Print Concealing the 'Ugly' Truth

The fine print on the labels of food products comprises nutritional facts per serving or per 100 g, including calories, total fat, cholesterol, carbs, proteins, etc. Therefore, people usually get tricked into believing that the entire product contains only a small amount of calories, sodium or trans-fats. So, if you buy a 500 g packet of salted snacks or 500 ml of aerated beverage, then do not forget to work out the math.

Moreover, at the bottom, the fine print also includes ingredients that have been used to make the product, for example, peanut butter, dextrose (sweetener), corn syrup, hydrogenated oils and other additives like emulsifiers and stabilizers. But this information is printed in such a small font that it escapes the attention of the customer. And secondly, companies do not find it necessary to describe the emulsifiers, preservatives or stabilizers they are using. This is because it is not mandatory to do so. Therefore, a food company might be taking an emulsifier derived from an animal source and using it in a product that is perceived as safe to be consumed by vegetarians.

Further, a food company only indicates the usage of Class II preservatives but never mentions the composition and combination of actual preservatives that it has used. So, the question we need to ask ourselves is, *'Do we ever look into*

cancer hazards, *International Journal of Occupational and Environmental Health*, 2007.

the chemicals that comprise the Class II preservatives?'

The list includes benzoates, sorbates, nitrites, glycerides, etc. Though they are stamped as safe to be consumed by Food Safety and Standards Authority of India, they are permissible in extremely small quantities. We do not realize that the amount of these products we consume on a daily basis is appallingly dangerous and hazardous to our health.

We purchase these products in bulk thinking they have an extended shelf-life but end up consuming them quickly. This is where companies make more profit as they ease us into buying their products in large volumes repeatedly.

4. Visibility of the product at a store

What do you see first when you enter the food section of a supermarket? I am sure the answer is cookies, biscuits, chips, fruit cake, bread, instant noodles, tea and coffee. It is because these products have high-profit margins. They are displayed at the eye level to promote visibility and accessibility. Moreover, the usage of colours like red and yellow on the packaging catches the attention of the customer.

The Size Matters

At any supermarket, bigger-sized food packets are immaculately placed on the shelves such that they immediately grab our attention. Smaller packets are usually kept behind or placed at the corners. Consequently, we end up buying the food packets of bigger size. However, we consume the contents of the bigger packets at a similar rate as that of the smaller ones. As a result, we go back to buying the same product the next week.

For instance, a 750 ml bottle of coke is most likely to be

consumed in one go as a 200 ml bottle would be. Even if we share 750 ml with one or two people, we are most likely to drink more coke than we would have had we bought a 200 ml bottle, which we would have consumed by ourselves.

The attempt to lure a customer does not end there. Have you realized how much you buy from the section behind the cash counter? This section mostly includes small consumable items like candies, chocolates, bread and other sweet foods, especially to attract children.

The Health Section Illusion

A few supermarkets are now adopting a strategy of having a separate 'health' section inside the food aisle. This section includes multigrain food, supplements and products that are cereal-based or milk-based, which are deemed healthy.

These stores try to create an illusion of stepping into a magical place where we can meet all our health requirements. As a result, we are lured into buying these products thinking that they are different. And yes, a few of these products are indeed beneficial for our health but not all of them because of the reasons highlighted earlier. Ironically, you won't find fresh fruits and vegetables in this section. They will be kept separately in the 'fruits and vegetables' section.

5. Health comes at a price

Remember how Sabrina looked at the price of whole almonds and then dropped the idea of buying it. What she noticed was the cost of almonds and compared it with the amount she would have to pay on buying a bunch of salted snacks and potatoes instead.

The reason behind the comparison was right. We pay ₹65–70 for a packet of branded potato chips weighing 170–200 g. If we bring it to 1 kg, we have to pay approximately ₹350. On the contrary, almonds per kg amount to ₹700–900 roughly. Likewise, 100 ml of olive oil might cost around ₹150; whereas you can purchase 1 litre of refined oil at approximately ₹120.

Similarly, if you buy non-branded whole milk directly from a cattle farmer, you might have to pay him around ₹60 for cow milk and ₹80 for buffalo milk. Whereas a 1 litre bottle of a soft drink will cost you ₹45–50, depending upon the brand. Yogurt is even more expensive. A branded pack of yogurt weighing 200 g can cost about ₹40.

However, we don't weigh in the health benefits that olive oil, almonds or yogurt offers us for that price. We certainly do not even remotely consider medical expenses that we might have to bear if we continue consuming unhealthy snacks and sugary aerated drinks.

FOOD FOR THOUGHT

If the cost of olive oil, almonds or whole milk seems to be a lot, try imagining how much you spend on monthly alcohol and smoking. Surely, whiskey and cigarettes neither satiate your appetite nor provide any health benefit.

So, can't you cut down your unnecessary expenses to buy more healthy products?

Which state would you rather picture yourself in?

- Obese, lying idle on the couch and not being able to move without pain and enjoy the world outside or
- Active, smiling, having a fit body and playing with your kids and grandchildren.

6. No time for health

Rabhya buys the food that is ready-to-eat or quick to prepare, not caring about its adverse health effects. The only good thing that Rabhya buys is eggs. And that's the similar kind of food preferences students have these days, living in hostels and as paying guests. Furthermore, young professionals living alone also prefer such foods.

What we don't understand is that there is a reason why we can prepare certain packed foods in two to three minutes. The presence of certain ingredients helps them get cooked instantly; those very ingredients induce heavy metal toxicity inside our bodies. Multiple studies done in the past decade indicate the presence of heavy metal and other toxicities in instant noodles and cereal-based food products.[6] [7]

The story does not end here. In addition to eating packed foods, people living alone, students and those working in night shifts have been increasingly ordering food from online platforms. Working extra hours, sleeping till late and then rushing to work leave them with no time to prepare fresh food. Though ordering food from restaurants helps in satiating hunger quickly, we do not know about certain things like:

- The type of oil used for cooking
- Quality and sourcing of ingredients used

[6]Md Saiful Islam, Md Kawser Ahmed, and Md Habibullah-Al-Mamun, 'Heavy Metals in Cereals and Pulses: Health Implications in Bangladesh', *Journal of Agricultural and Food Chemistry*, 13 October 2014.

[7]Sonomdagva Chonokhuu, Chultem Batbold, Byambatseren Chuluunpurev et al., 'Contamination and Health Risk Assessment of Heavy Metals in the Soil of Major Cities in Mongolia', *International Journal of Environmental Research and Public Health*, 17 July 2019.

- The freshness of the pre-cooked food
- The kind of conditions wherein people cook the food, and
- The type of packaging material used

In other words, we have no idea about the standards of hygiene maintained in the kitchen where the food is being prepared.

7. Not exploring healthier options in supermarket

When we go to the market to buy new furniture or new clothes, we examine the product thoroughly. We invest a lot of time in reviewing different varieties and asking many questions before zeroing down on one product. But do we do the same while purchasing food? Do we spend as much time exploring healthier options as we spend checking varieties while shopping for furniture or garments?

You have to remember that the same shelves with packets of refined corn oil or sunflower oil also have other cooking oils like olive oil and edible coconut oil, kept beside them. There are not only apples, mangoes and bananas but also melons, cantaloupes and guava present in the supermarket. The latter fruits are as tasty and much healthier and do not spike up blood sugar level atypically. By all means, one can have apple once or twice a week, but, fruits with a low glycemic load (GL)[8] like melons, avocado and berries are much better.

The family of cruciferous vegetables, which includes cabbage, cauliflower and broccoli, offers a few of the healthiest foods produced by nature. But how many of us are consuming them regularly in a week? Ginger and garlic offer loads of

---

[8]Glycemic load indicates the amount of carbohydrate present per serving of the food.

vitamins in relatively small quantities. But do we buy them as enthusiastically as we purchase onions, tomatoes and potatoes?

FOOD FOR THOUGHT

You must be aware of various brands selling refined flours and can surely identify them in a supermarket. However, do you know about a single brand selling whole-grain or gluten-free flour?

Are we including ginger and garlic in significant amounts in our every meal? Or are we using them seldom and sparingly?

8. International health guidelines

Most of the international guidelines for food have become obsolete. The guidelines are still the same as they were in 1970s when glucose (carbohydrate) was considered the most prominent source of energy. All kinds of fats were labeled villains. Guidelines recommended that over 50 per cent of the energy intake in a diet should be coming from carbohydrates and dietary fat consumption be reduced to 30 per cent.

However, since then, studies have shown that naturally occurring fat is healthy and produces more energy than glucose after getting metabolized.[9] [10] This kind of healthy fat is present in non-processed seed oils, milk, organic butter, seafood, meat,

---

[9]David L. Nelson and Cox M. M, *Lehninger Principles of Biochemistry,* 7th edition, 2017.

[10]Imamura F., Micha R., Wu J.H.Y., de Oliveira Otto MC., et al., 'Effects of Saturated Fat, Polyunsaturated Fat, Monounsaturated Fat, and Carbohydrate on Glucose-Insulin Homeostasis: A Systematic Review and Meta-analysis of Randomised Controlled Feeding Trials', PLoS Med 13(7), 2016, https://journals.plos.org/plosmedicine/article?id=10.1371/journal.pmed.1002087. Accessed on 19 December 2021.

vegetables and fruits like avocado, etc. Also, advancements in biochemistry have proved that carbohydrates metabolize into fats, posing a risk of getting obesity and cardiometabolic disorders.

The initial sets of guidelines were formulated without collecting enough scientific evidence. Today, researchers say that they should not have been issued publicly in the first place. These misleading guidelines created a surge in carbohydrate intake and decreased fat consumption in people's diets. The most prominent mistake on the part of guidelines was that these did not clearly distinguish naturally occurring healthy fat from industrially processed unhealthy trans-fats. Also, they did not make any distinction between complex carbohydrates— with dietary fibre, proven to be beneficial for our gut—and simple carbohydrates, causing inflammation in our body, resulting in chronic diseases and comorbidities.

It is noteworthy that most of the international health institutes are funded by the same food companies that produce aerated soft drinks, instant noodles, bread, milk, cookies and chips. Therefore, it is not surprising that these guidelines recommend including most of these products in your diet as a source of carbohydrate and quick energy.

Dieticians all over the world have figured out that high fat diet with low-carb content is best suited for our body. They are recommending consuming only 25-30 g carbohydrates and that too in the form of dietary fibre which is present in only naturally occurring fruits and vegetables, not in chips, cookies and soft drinks.

9. Weighing benefits of exercise over diet

When we think of a lean, slim and fit body, we mostly relate it with exercising and hitting the gym. However, the truth is that the diet contributes 80 per cent towards our healthy body, and exercise only 20 per cent. Most of us think that we can compensate for overeating sugar by doing specific physical activities, but that's a wrong approach. The amount of calories we consume in eating a single meal with high carbohydrate content cannot be burned with a single day of exercising lasting only 60 minutes.

Exercise is only beneficial for building muscular strength, and that too requires following a proper, healthy and nutritious diet. Otherwise, we don't necessarily have to spend our hard-earned money on fitness facilities to remain healthy and in good shape.

CONCLUSION

What we think while selecting the food we buy is based on what has been directed to our subconscious by the constant influx of misleading information, advertisements and peer influences. Additionally, lack of time to cook fresh food for ourselves and not wanting to spend a few extra bucks on much healthier food do more harm than good to our body.

It's all about developing a habit.

Just as we have developed a habit of eating junk food, we can also cultivate the habit of eating healthy and wholesome food. We can work on avoiding future medical expenses.

Currently, our food choices are influenced by what's being supplied, visible and accessible to us instead of what should be there on our kitchen shelves. Otherwise, we would have had more vegetables for salads in our refrigerator, more almonds and pistachios than packets of instant-noodles and chips in our kitchen racks and more melons, kiwi, berries and papayas than boxes of industrially-processed fruit juices.

2

THE IMPACT OF OUR CURRENT FOOD CHOICES

We have so far discussed that factors like advertisements impact our subconscious in making food choices. Meanwhile, social status, peer influence, money and time constraints drive us to make conscious decisions when it comes to trying a certain cuisine, consuming ready-to-eat food or buying cheap, unhealthy items.

So, a few obvious follow-up questions that you might think of can be:

- How does it matter what we consume?
- What happens when we regularly eat foods with a lot of refined sugar or simple carbohydrates?
- Why are industrially processed and refined products unhealthy for us and how do they affect our overall well-being?
- Why and how is it beneficial to consume non-refined seed oils, whole-grain flours, fresh fruits and vegetables?

Therefore, it is extremely crucial to acquire further clarity. We will extend the discussion we had in the previous chapter by simultaneously addressing the issues mentioned above.

But before we delve further into how our current food choices affect our gut and overall health, it's imperative to understand some basic terms pertaining to particular conditions.

- **Hyperglycemia**: A persistent state of high levels of glucose in the bloodstream that can eventually cause inflammation and increase the risk of developing diabetes and other chronic ailments.
- **Insulin response**: Pancreas secretes insulin as a response to increased glucose build-up in the blood after consuming a meal. Insulin signals the cells to uptake glucose from the bloodstream for generating energy.
- **Insulin resistance:** This is a chronic state that develops inside the body secondary to prolonged hyperglycemia, wherein cells stop responding to the insulin. As cells become resistant to insulin, they stop taking enough glucose, leading to the build-up of blood sugar levels.
- **Hyperinsulinemia**: This is a chronic state resulting from the development of insulin resistance. As cells stop responding to the insulin signals, the pancreas tries to over-compensate by secreting higher amounts of insulin. This state of hyperinsulinemia then evokes an inflammatory response from various organ networks, including the immune, cardiac and nervous systems.
- **Inflammation:** This is a critical but non-specific defense reaction to any tissue injury.
- **Chronic low-grade/silent inflammation:** This is a kind of inflammation that develops as a result of the persistent response from the immune system over a prolonged period to fight oxidative stress, repair the damage to the organ linings or eliminate heavy metal toxicity, etc. It's referred to as 'low-grade' or 'silent' because it does not straightaway produce any visible response that can be felt or seen like

developing a fever in case of viral infection, redness of the skin as an allergic reaction or diarrhoea and vomiting in case of gastrointestinal infection by a bacteria. However, as the inflammation persists, it leads to developing a wide array of disorders, including Type-2 diabetes, hypertension, rheumatoid arthritis, depression, dementia, etc.

(Going ahead in this book, the term inflammation would imply the chronic 'low-grade' inflammation.)

- **Cardiometabolic syndrome**: It is a syndrome with metabolic dysfunction, characterized by insulin resistance and inflammation. It encompasses comorbidities like diabetes, dyslipidemia, hypertension and fatty liver disease.
- **Insulin sensitivity:** It is the opposite of insulin resistivity and refers to how sensitive cells in the body are responding towards the released insulin. The more insulin sensitive the cells are, the more effectively they are going to take up the sugar from the blood, thereby preventing the state of hyperglycemia and thus diabetes.
- **Triglycerides (TGL):** They are the most common type of fat, a form in which the excess amount of sugars and calories are stored. Its high levels damage blood vessels, cause obesity and promote inflammation. Moreover, they inhibit the production of high-density lipoprotein cholesterol (HDL-c).
- **Low-Density Lipoprotein cholesterol (LDL-c):** This cholesterol reverses the damage done by triglycerides to the arteries by sticking on the arterial walls. As LDL-c keeps on getting deposited on to the walls, the arteries begin to get blocked resulting in atherosclerosis and increased risk of a heart attack. Although LDL-c acts as a bandage to protect blood vessels, their sticky property has got them the disrepute of 'bad' cholesterol.

- **HDL-c:** It serves as a transporter carrying LDL-c from arteries and cells to the liver, from where the LDL-c is flushed out. Since it helps in eliminating LDL-c, it diminishes the risk of heart diseases and hence is regarded as 'good' cholesterol.

THE 'LOAD' OF A HIGH GLYCEMIC LOAD FOOD

Without getting confused with more medical jargon, let's try to comprehend what glycemic load or GL is and how it shapes our health. In simple words, GL indicates the amount of carbohydrates present per serving of the food, thus helping in determining how much quantity of a particular food we should consume in a day.

GL of less than 10 is considered low, and that equal to or higher than 20 is critically high. Foods with a high GL spike up your blood sugar levels, posing a more prominent risk of contributing towards hyperglycemia and hence insulin resistance.

- Foods with GL lesser than or equal to 10 are considered excellent and can be consumed in moderate amounts daily. For example, 100 g serving of watermelon has very low GL of 4.
- Foods with GL of 11–19 should be consumed in a limited amount for about two to three times a week. One cup of oatmeal with yogurt can have a GL of 12–15 depending upon the proportions of oats and yogurt in the meal.
- Foods with GL greater than or equal to 20 possess a high risk of contributing towards hyperglycemia, insulin resistance and obesity, leading to the cardiometabolic

syndrome. Avoid such foods as much as possible. For example, a regular serving of baked potato has a GL of 28. One cup of white rice has 33.

Other foods with high GL that we consume regularly, but should avoid include

- White bread, pizza, pasta, hot rice and hot/baked potatoes
- Bananas, dates, grapes, lychee and dried fruits like dates, raisins, prunes and figs
- Fried chicken, French fries, chips, candy, cookies, pastries, ice cream and chocolates
- Beer, sweetened beverages (aerated drinks, lemonade, and iced tea), energy drinks and fruit alcohol
- Biscuits, ketchup and other confectionary items

There is another concept making rounds on the internet to determine how sugary a food item is. It is known as Glycemic Index (GI). It indicates how quickly and by what level your blood sugar will elevate after consuming the said food as compared to eating pure glucose. The GI measure ranks food on a scale of 0 to 100 with 0–55 being considered to have low sugars. Foods having GI value of more than 70 are considered having high sugar content. Nutritionists, however, are now discouraging the use of GI as a marker to indicate how much carbohydrate content a food item contains. It is because GI does not take into account the portion of the food we consume, which thus does not indicate the actual amount of carbohydrates taken.

For example, the GI of watermelon is 72, which is extremely high. But are we going to eat an entire watermelon at once? It is where GL comes into the picture. GL of watermelon is a mere four per 100 g serving, indicating that watermelon is quite safe to consume regularly, and is good even for people with diabetes.

Similarly, the GL of one cup of oatmeal comes out to be 12–15 indicating one should only consume one cup of it only two to three times a week. On the contrary, GI of oatmeal, which falls between 55–58, will mislead you to have oatmeal daily, never telling you how much to eat.

Takeaway: Always search for the GL of foods per serving on credible websites or visit a nutritionist to get an idea about how much carbs you're going to get from consuming a particular food.

BEWARE OF THE WHITES!

White-coloured foods are the ones that are industrially processed and refined. These 'whites' include refined flour, white sandwich bread, white rice, pizza, pasta, table sugar, etc. They get their whitish colour through the process of refinement which removes their outer layer where dietary fibre is located. As the fibre is removed, all that is left in terms of carbs are simple sugar molecules, which our body absorbs relatively quickly and causes the blood glucose to spike immediately.

Increased blood sugars evoke an insulin response from the pancreas. Ordinarily, insulin signals the cells to uptake sugar from the blood to convert them into energy for general functioning and carrying on metabolic activities. However, as insulin keeps signalling the cells over long periods continuously, the cells gradually become inefficient in responding. It causes blood sugar levels to remain high and rise as we eat, eventually developing diabetes.

The main problem with eating white-coloured foods or

following a diet with high GL is that the high amounts of carbs that are absorbed in the body do not entirely get metabolized into energy. More than 50 per cent of the carbs are converted into fats that get deposited and stored beneath the superficial muscle cells, making them swell, eventually causing obesity.

Furthermore, the large proportions of simple sugars present in the white-coloured foods and others with a high GL serve as a feed for harmful bacteria in the gut, regarding which we will discuss in detail in the next part of the book.

REFINING FOOD HAS NOT REFINED OUR HEALTH

Wholegrain, botanically, is a seed of a plant with its coating intact. The seed coat consists of the bran and germ, which contain most of the nutritious value of the grain. The process of refining strips off the bran and germ makes it lose about 25 per cent of its protein and a significant proportion of several essential nutrients. Although products are enriched back with some vitamins and minerals, their proportions are significantly diminished in comparison to that in the pure whole grain.

The story does not end with refining just the grains, but extends to extracting oils from plants and seeds as well. Refined oils go through a chemical process called hydrogenation, which is why they are also called partially hydrogenated oils (PHOs). While the oils are hydrogenated or refined, the chemical structure of natural fatty acids changes to form trans-fats.

The trans-fats have become an integral component of PHO that are produced intentionally as they affect the properties of the oil, increasing its melting point and shelf life. Furthermore, the trans-fats enhance the flavour stability of the oil, altering the characteristics of the food to which it is added.

These industrially produced artificial trans-fats are hazardous to health. Upon consumption with the food, they

- Increase LDL-c significantly without raising HDL-c, lowering cardiac and liver health and elevating the risk of artery blockage and fatty liver disease
- Promote prominent inflammation in the gut and other organs, serving as a primary underlying cause of many chronic ailments, including obesity, cancer, hypertension arthritis, etc.
- Diminish insulin sensitivity in the cells, therefore, increasing insulin resistivity and thus posing the risk of developing diabetes

DID YOU KNOW?

The trans-fats are a type of TGL. Hence, regular consumption of foods and oils with artificial or industrially produced trans-fats increases the TGL levels like no other food. TGL alone can act as a significant risk factor for obesity and heart attack. The medications that help decrease cholesterol levels are not effective in reducing TGL levels. Hence, dietary control is the only measure to avoid coronary heart disease, heart attack or any other cardiovascular disease.

These unhealthy fats are only found in industrially processed foods that are hydrogenated to increase their shelf lives, impart flavour stability and add a crunchy texture to them. Some prominent examples include popcorns, biscuits, packed cereals, pizzas, chips, cookies, refined oils and ice creams. And if you did not expect ice creams to be included in this list, then you're in for an unpleasant surprise.

It is the hydrogenated fat that provides consistency and structural stability to ice-creams. In short, the trans-fats are extremely bad fats.

They are so harmful that World Health Organization has called out for an extensive strategy to eliminate trans-fat from the global food supply by 2023. In the United States, the Food and Drug Administration had given a ruling in 2015, which stated, 'Artificial trans-fats were unsafe to eat'. The administration gave three years to food companies to eliminate these detrimental fats from their food items.[11]

A NOTE ON OUR CURRENT FOOD CHOICES

With the consumption of noodles, rolls made of refined flour, fried foods in refined oil, cookies, cakes and other processed and packed food items, all we have been eating are junk foods, thus putting our bodies under heavy GL. As we keep putting more unhealthy carbs and trans-fats into our bodies, we put ourselves in the line of getting obese and predispose our bodies towards increased cardiovascular risks.

Refined foods/whites → heavy glycemic load → hyperglycemia → insulin resistance → inflammation → obesity and more inflammation → metabolic syndrome→ increased cardiovascular risks

The temptation to eat palatable and delicious food is understandable. However, we need to substitute our junk food

---

[11]'Artificial Trans Fats Banned in US', *Harvard T.H. Chan School of Public Health,* https://www.hsph.harvard.edu/news/hsph-in-the-news/us-bans-artificial-trans-fats/. Accessed on 19 December 2021.

with healthier carbs, keeping the softness and sweetness intact in our diet.

IS IT THAT SIMPLE OR COMPLEX?

Carbohydrates and sugars are two terms that are used interchangeably. Typically, carbohydrates can be categorized as either simple carbohydrates that are simple sugars, mostly tasting sweet or complex 'starchy' carbohydrates (sugars+starch+dietary fibre). Chemically, they are different in terms of the length of their sugar chains and how they are prearranged with dietary fibre or starch or both.

Simple carbs consist of sugars of shorter lengths. Our body systems digest and absorb them quickly, using them as a significant source of immediate energy. On the contrary, complex carbs are made of longer sugar chains, accompanied by starch and dietary fibre, which do not allow the carbohydrate chain to break down easily. Instead, they ensure that some amount of carbs remain undigested and reach the colon (large intestine), where it serves as a feed for beneficial bacteria. Hence, one will get fewer amounts of sugar released at a more consistent rate. Vegetables and whole grains are the best sources of complex carbs.

If you're wondering about which carbs to go for, then you've got to embrace both simple and complex, but in their naturally occurring form. It should be done because...

- **The complex can be turned into simple**
  Almost all packed food items, through the process of refining, have dietary fibre removed from their natural ingredients while stripping off their outer coatings. It implies that carbs are broken down in the body more

rapidly, raising the blood sugar levels similarly to how simple sugars do.

- **And simple can impart complex effects**
  On the other hand, fruits might contain simple carbs, but many of them carry plenty of dietary fibre. The dietary fibre changes the way the body processes the sugars and slows down their digestion, making them act more like complex carbohydrates.

  Simple sugars alone serve as a feed for toxic bacteria living in the gut, causing inflammation. However, when dietary fibre is present along with them, it shifts the balance towards the growth of good bacteria inside the gut, preventing inflammation, cleansing the colon and facilitating the removal of toxicities.

  Therefore, naturally occurring simple carbs and whole foods containing complex carbs are relatively safe to consume. They are a much healthier alternative to industrially processed food with added sweeteners and preservatives.

OUR DEFICIENT DIET

There are a few elements that are essential as nutrition for the body to function correctly and carry out a wide range of specific tasks. These elements serve as micronutrients as our bodies require them in lesser quantities in comparison to protein, carbohydrate and fats. They are broadly categorized as vitamins and minerals, catalysing the execution of various metabolic reactions and maintaining certain health conditions. For example, vitamins boost immunity, improve vision health, repair damaged cells and DNA and facilitate in performing many other functions. Similarly, minerals like calcium, phosphorus, iron, zinc, copper and others serve a spectrum of purposes, ranging from improving blood circulation and bone density to promoting cardiovascular health and cognitive functioning.

One aspect of our diet that creates a subtle but long-lasting impact on our health is the micronutrient deficiency in it. Whether it is street food or veggies prepared at home with roti or rice or something at a fancy restaurant, we are not taking in enough of the essential micronutrients, even though they are required in trace amounts. They play a vital role in developing our immunity, promoting health of the organs and treating inflammation in the body. And more importantly, they exhibit antioxidant properties.

A SHORT NOTE ON ANTIOXIDANT PROPERTIES

An antioxidant is a compound that inhibits oxidation. Most of the micronutrients and many naturally occurring bioactive molecules in plants serve as antioxidants exhibiting specific properties. Plenty of essential metabolic processes occurring inside the body produce free radicals as a by-product. These free radicals are highly reactive species that engage with healthy cells and put them under oxidative stress, disrupting their cellular integrity. It leads to permanent cellular damage and abnormal cell death, which in turn causes inflammation, promotes tumour growth and develops the risk of cancer.

Antioxidants prevent free radicals from interacting with healthy cells by actively neutralizing them, implying that they significantly reduce the risk of cancer and other chronic ailments like cardiometabolic syndrome. Furthermore, they impart a spectrum of health benefits.

BACK TO THE MICRONUTRIENT DEFICIENCY

Except for a couple of vitamins, our body cannot synthesize micronutrients and thus requires them to be consumed through the food we eat. And here's the good news! We can meet their requirement conveniently if we include fruits and vegetables in our diet as they are not present in packed/refined products and street foods.

Since vitamins and minerals are not required in abundance and are often not talked about in the same capacity as proteins, carbs or fats, they are often neglected in our diet. But their deficiency can lead to serious health implications that can prove to be lethal in the longer run. These include

- Persistent clinical fatigue: A person will always remain lethargic and feel demotivated, which can lead to stress, and in extreme cases, depression.
- Hormonal imbalance and metabolic dysfunction
- Predisposition to cardiovascular diseases, diabetes and hypertension
- Inflammation, leading to metabolic syndrome and autoimmune diseases like rheumatoid arthritis, inflammatory bowel disease, and Type 1 diabetes etc.
- Increased risk of developing neurological disorders like dementia and Alzheimer's

Let's explore the deficiency of most important micronutrients and their related chronic implications in brief.

TABLE 1
List of micronutrients and their health impact

Micronutrients	Primary roles	Consequence of deficiency
Vitamin A	• Improves vision, skin and health of hair • Exhibits strong antioxidant attributes, promotes cardiac health • Supports the immune system • Anti-inflammatory in nature, important in normal functioning of kidney, liver and lungs • Contributes to reducing the risk of acne and metabolic syndrome • Increases longevity and promotes reproductive health	• Weakening of the eyesight and night blindness • Impaired immunity and getting microbial infections frequently • Dry skin and acne • Increased risk of suffering from chronic ailments
Vitamin B1	• Proper functioning of cardiac, GI, and nervous systems • Maintaining mental health	• Beriberi disease • Loss of appetite • Fatigue, frustration and agitation
Vitamin B2	• Boosts energy levels • Critical in development of the baby inside womb • Cellular growth and development • Hormone production and regulation	• Mood swings • Fatigue and weakness • Anaemia

Micronutrients	Primary roles	Consequence of deficiency
Vitamin B3	• Integral to synthesis of DNA and repairing DNA damage • Facilitates cell signalling • Acts as antioxidant • Boosts cognitive function • Exhibits potent anti-inflammatory activities, preventing rheumatoid arthritis and Type 1 diabetes • Regulates cholesterol and triglyceride levels	• Memory loss and cognitive decline • Depression • Skin issues • Decline in liver and cardiac health
Vitamin B6 and B12	• Critical for neural health	• Dementia and Alzheimer's
Vitamin B9	• Vital for foetus development • Maintaining normal levels of serotonin	• Neural tube defects in foetus that can lead to cognitive impairment in a developing child • Clinical depression
Vitamin C	• Exhibits potent antiviral and other antimicrobial properties, thus vital in boosting the immunity • Anti-inflammatory in nature and serves as a powerful antioxidant • Increases longevity • Absorption of iron • Maintenance of connective tissues and bone health	• Scurvy and easy bruising • Muscle weakness and fatigue • Impaired immunity and getting microbial infections frequently • Anaemia and exhaustion

Micronutrients	Primary roles	Consequence of deficiency
Vitamin D	• Helps the body to absorb calcium and regulate calcium-phosphorus levels • Promotes bone health • Maintaining normal functions of the immune system • Stimulates the activity of beneficial neurotransmitters, uplifting the mood • Improves insulin sensitivity, reducing the risk of Type 2 diabetes	• Frequently getting sick or infected • Muscle and bone pain • Prone to spine disorders • Physical and mental fatigue • Low mood • Increased risk of developing autoimmune disorders like rheumatoid arthritis
Vitamin E	• Potent antioxidant, boosting immunity and promoting neural health	• Loss of muscle coordination • Weakened immune system
Vitamin K	• Normal blood clotting • Improves bone metabolism • Regulates blood calcium levels	• Abnormal bleeding and haemorrhages
Calcium	• Strengthens muscles and bones • Integral to proper growth of the body • Improves cardiac functioning and helps blood vessels to constrict and relax	• Bone weakness, increased risk of fracture and osteoporosis • Improves blood pressure

Micronutrients	Primary roles	Consequence of deficiency
Phosphorus	• Promotes bone health • Improves nerve conduction and maintaining neural health • DNA repair and proper growth of the body	• Physical fatigue • Joint stiffness and osteoporosis
Iron	• Vital in synthesis of haemoglobin, which carries oxygen from lungs to other tissues, thus sustaining life and maintaining basic cellular and metabolic activities • Carries out energy metabolism, required to make energy molecules • Promotes cognitive health	• Anaemia • Fatigue, headaches and dizziness • Shortness of breath and heart palpitations
Zinc	• Drives metabolisms of protein, lipids and carbohydrates • Promotes bone health • Helps in wound healing • Improves cognitive function	• Reduced reproductive function • Anaemia • Mental retardation • Delayed wound healing and suppression of immunity

Micronutrients	Primary roles	Consequence of deficiency
Magnesium	• Regulates blood pressure, improves cardiac health • Critical in maintaining mental and cognitive health and improving learning • Promotes muscle and bone health • Anti-inflammatory in nature • Boosts the immunity • Improves insulin metabolism and controls glucose levels	• Increased mental fatigue and sensitivity to stress, which can lead to depression or anxiety • Hypertension (elevated BP) • Muscle weakness and osteoporosis • Chronic inflammation • Increased risk of diabetes
Manganese	• Facilitates and drives the metabolism of lipids and carbs • Promoting bone health • Boosting immunity • Maintaining and improving reproductive health	• Increased risk of osteoporosis • Chronic fatigue, headache and loss of vigour • Can lead to development of impotence
Selenium	• Serves as an antioxidant, exhibiting anti-carcinogenic activities • Significant in proper functioning of thyroid gland	• Increased risk of central nervous system disorders and cancer • Hypothyroidism
Copper	• Improves blood count • Promotes bone health • Strengthens connective tissues	• Anaemia • Bone abnormalities • Increased risk of osteoporosis

Micronutrients	Primary roles	Consequence of deficiency
Iodine	• Critical for synthesis of thyroid hormones (T3 and T4)	• Goitre • Hypothyroidism
Molybdenum	• Carries out uric acid and amino acids metabolisms	• Elevated uric acid levels, leading to gout
Cobalt	• Associated with Vitamin B12 • Improves blood count	• Anaemia
Chromium	• Vital for carrying out metabolism of protein, lipids and carbs • Promotes bone health	• Liver and kidney dysfunction • Increased risk of central nervous system disorder

Given the fact that every micronutrient plays a critical role in maintaining and promoting a certain aspect of health, especially when a lot of them serve as antioxidants and exhibit anti-inflammatory properties, their deficiency in our daily diet turns our bodies into a living wreck. It makes us susceptible to get hit by chronic diseases and infected by a plethora of pathogens.

FROM DEFICIENCY OF THE ESSENTIALS TO INCORPORATING POISON

In chemistry, most of the minerals are grouped as metals. These metals include iron, zinc, fluoride, iodine, manganese, molybdenum, selenium, copper, cobalt and chromium. They play a significant role as 'helper molecules' in carrying out activities of enzymes, maintaining cellular processes, balancing hormonal levels, etc.

While our bodily systems need these elements in trace amounts, there are a few heavy metals that we do not require at all as they do not impart any functional effects. These heavy metals include mercury (Hg), lead (Pb), cadmium (Cd) and arsenic (As). These, when consumed and absorbed by soft tissues, have a critical effect on the gut microbiome, severely impacting the GI tract and overall gut stability. Our gut microbiome comprises trillions of bacteria living in the lower part of the intestine that affect our health.

Heavy metal toxicity

Heavy metals enter our food chain through various routes like fertilizers and pesticides, polluted water and soil used in agriculture and toxic waste eaten by sea animals that we consume as seafood. When consumed, they bind to the healthy tissues and induce toxicities inside the gut and in various other organs.

Overall, the heavy metal load diminishes longevity, predisposes us to chronic ailments and increases the risk of developing cancer. For example, metals like mercury and lead cause damage to DNA, gastrointestinal poisoning, along with neurological and kidney toxicities. Whereas, metals like arsenic and cadmium impart significant changes to the gut microbiome by suppressing the growth of probiotic bacteria associated with metabolic health. More potential toxic effects of heavy metals are listed below.

Mercury (Hg)

- The organic form of mercury (methyl-mercury) induces neurotoxicity in young children, hindering brain and cognitive development. Methyl-mercury can also cross the placental barrier, causing brain damage in the unborn baby, which can then lead to impaired learning and speech difficulties in the developing child.

- Induces neurotoxicity, exhibiting lack of coordination and muscle control
- Causes muscle weakness
- Causes hearing and speech difficulties
- Damages the kidneys

Lead (Pb)

- Can cause paralysis, also referred to as lead palsy
- Induces anaemia
- Imparts damage to the reproductive organs and kidneys
- Weakens the immune system
- Causes memory loss

Cadmium (Cd)

- Induces toxicity to the kidneys
- Affects liver health by inhibiting the production of bile acids
- Causes damage to the lungs, resulting in breathing problems and predisposing people to lung tumours

Arsenic (As)

- Acts as a carcinogenic agent, increasing the risk of cancer
- Found to be associated with causing skin inflammation
- Induces nausea, vomiting and diarrhoea
- Affects the cardiovascular system, developing irregular heart rhythm

Have a look at the list below to find some common food sources that can induce heavy metal toxicities, when consumed regularly.

TABLE 2

Food sources inducing toxicities	Heavy metal toxicity
• Juices and packed products with emulsifiers • Instant food	Lead and cadmium
• Rice, especially brown rice	Cadmium and arsenic
• Fish and shellfish, like swordfish and marlin • Offal (liver and kidney) of animal foods	Mercury, lead and cadmium
• Mussels, oysters and scallops	Cadmium
• Crab, meat (white meat>brown meat) • Shellfish, molluscs and seaweeds	Arsenic
• Alcohol	Increases the absorption of heavy metals (particularly cadmium) inside the body

Heavy metal as carcinogens

Apart from all the adversities listed above, the most dreadful impact that heavy metals can create in our bodies is causing cancer. Increased exposure to heavy metals through diet or physical environment can lead to their accumulation in the blood in toxic amounts. When absorbed by the intestine, these heavy metals act as potential carcinogens[12] by causing mutagenic changes in the DNA, exhibiting oxidative stress and promoting abnormal cellular growth resulting in the formation of a benign tumour and later turning into a malignant form (known as cancer).

One can comprehend how heavy metals cause an increased risk of chronic ailments by analysing the prevalence of these

---

[12]A substance capable of causing cancer in living tissue.

disorders in the areas where people get exposed to them in their working and living environments. For example,

- There is a significantly increased prevalence of pancreatic cancer and non-Hodgkin's lymphoma in the areas where people get exposed to contaminated soil with arsenic.
- Studies have associated cancers of the stomach, prostate and lungs with people exposed to getting high emissions of cadmium, working in the mining industry.[13] [14]
- Mercury poisoning has been strongly linked to eating more seafood. People living around coastal areas are more exposed to eating fish and seafood. Studies have correlated increased mercury exposure with liver, renal and gastric cancer.[15]

FOODS DISGUISED AS 'HEALTHY'

Food companies boast about plenty of their products, claiming to be imparting a wide range of health benefits. They promote them as superfoods in the advertisements. These foods are slightly expensive than the usual products and placed at separate shelves to make them stand out from the rest in the supermarket. These products include fruit juices with 'loads

---

[13]Austin Carver and Vincent S. Gallicchio, 'Heavy Metals and Cancer', *IntechOpen*, 20 December 2017.

[14]James Huff, Ruth M. Lunn, Michael P. Waalkes, Lorenzo Tomatis, and Peter F. Infante, 'Cadmium-induced Cancers in Animals and in Humans', *International Journal of Occupational and Environmental Health*, 2007.

[15]Wenzhen Yuan, Ning Yang and Xiangkai Li, 'Advances in Understanding How Heavy Metal Pollution Triggers Gastric Cancer', *Biomed Research International*, 2016.

of vitamins', 'multi-grain' bread, cookies with 'digestive fibre', 'nutritious' oatmeal etc.

While they might be somewhat healthier than other processed and packed foods, the harsh truth is that they do not exhibit any significant health benefits that we think they do. Instead, some of them might harm our bodies in similar proportions as other products. The primary reason is the high amount of simple carbs that these products carry in the form of 'added sugars' or refined flours. The second factor is the proportions of the healthy elements with which the companies claim to enrich their products. The percentage of the micronutrients, multiple grains or digestive fibre included in these foods is so low that they cannot impart any significant health benefit.

The point is that you can enjoy the goodness of extra amounts of essential micronutrients and meet the daily requirements of digestive fibre without facing implications of added sugars. All you've got to do is simply substitute your fruit juices, processed dairy, multi-grain products and packed oatmeal with fresh fruits, green leafy vegetables, homemade yogurt, fermented foods and whole grains. This is what we are going to focus on moving forward in this book.

SUMMARIZING THE SCIENCE BEHIND THE IMPACT OF OUR CURRENT FOOD CHOICES

The 'whites', including refined grain flours, burden our organ systems with high GL. Refined and hydrogenated vegetable oils carry trans-fat, raising TGL and LDL cholesterol levels. Seafood, alcohol drinks and packed products with added preservatives and emulsifiers significantly increase the risk of heavy metal toxicities.

A flow chart was presented earlier in this chapter, depicting the effects of consuming refined food/whites, leading to increased cardiovascular risks. Let us understand the physiological sequence of events better, correlating the chart with the help of a real-life example.

Consuming one cup of cooked/fried white rice regularly
↓
Heavy GL of 33
↓
Frequently evoking an intense insulin response
↓
Persistent hyperglycemia
↓
Gradually developing insulin resistance
↓
'Low-grade' inflammation building up
↓
More amount of carbs stored as triglycerides
↓
Increased fat deposition
↓
Resulting in obesity
↓
More signs and symptoms of inflammation showing up
↓
Clinically getting diagnosed with diabetes
↓
Fits the criteria of metabolic syndrome
↓
Increased cardiovascular risks (hypertension, atherosclerosis and heart attack)

Vegetables and whole grains are the best sources of complex carbs. Fruits might contain simple carbs, but many of them carry plenty of dietary fibre. Fruits and vegetables contain loads of micronutrients and bioactive plant compounds that serve as antioxidants and exhibit anti-inflammatory properties. Antioxidants prevent free radicals from interacting with healthy cells by actively neutralizing them, implying that they significantly reduce the risk of cancer and other chronic ailments like cardiometabolic syndrome. Furthermore, they impart a spectrum of benefits promoting overall well-being and health of the organs.

Given the fact that every micronutrient plays a critical role in maintaining and promoting a particular aspect of health, their deficiency in our daily diet turns our bodies into a living wreck. It has made us prone to get hit by chronic diseases and infected by a plethora of pathogens.

IT'S ALL ABOUT MAKING A HABIT

We need to substitute fruit juices, processed dairy, multi-grain products and packed oatmeal with fresh fruits, green leafy vegetables, homemade yogurt, fermented foods and whole grains.

Part II

GUT HEALTH

3

FOOD CHOICES THAT OUR GUT HATES!

The gastrointestinal tract, also referred to as the gut, is a habitat of trillions of microorganisms including bacteria, yeast, fungi and viruses. This diversity makes the gut an incredibly complex microbiota, indirectly affecting every aspect of human health. The microbiome present in the gut environment that co-evolved with humans to be mutually beneficial is known as probiotic.

A healthy gut

- Promotes digestion
- Enables the absorption of minerals, vitamins and other micronutrients
- Stimulates the synthesis of healthy short fatty acid chains
- Helps to maintain a healthy skin, boosts our immune system for fighting a wide range of pathogens
- Removes heavy metal toxicity
- Regulates blood pressure
- Control blood sugar levels and lowers triglyceride levels
- Improves cognition, learning and memory
- Enhances mental and emotional well-being

On the other hand, an unhealthy gut catalyses the development of ailing conditions leading to a wide spectrum of disorders, affecting not only itself but also the heart, liver, lungs, kidneys, brain and mental health.

A valid question arises at this point—what makes our gut healthy or unhealthy?

The answer is simple—our food choices, our diet.

Studies have proven that the gut microbiome is developed within the first 1,000 days from the day we are born, but can be altered throughout the life depending upon the environment we live in and the food we eat.[16] [17] Our gut is a home for both good as well as pathogenic bacteria. Therefore, one specific type of food is beneficial for probiotic bacteria and other specific type of food is good for pathogenic bacteria.

Good bacteria (probiotics) thrive on

- Dietary fibres associated with complex carbohydrates
- Healthy fats and fatty acids

On the contrary, pathogenic bacteria feed upon

- Sugars and refined carbohydrates,
- Trans-fat (industrially synthesized fat)

OUR GUT HATES SUGARS

A diet high in sugars throws off the delicate balance within the gut microbiota in the favour of pathogenic bacteria,

---

[16]Eline van der Beek, 'Nutritional Programming and Later Life – The role of macronutrient quality during the first 1,000 days', *Sight & Life E-magazine*, 32(1), 2018, p: 46–52.

[17]Ruairi C Robertson, Amee R Manges, B Brett Finlay, Andrew J Prendergast, 'The Human Microbiome and Child Growth - First 1000 Days and Beyond', *Trends in Microbiology*, 2019.

resulting in their overgrowth hindering the growth of beneficial bacteria.

Diet rich in sugars
↓
Overgrowth of pathogenic bacteria
↓
Hindrance in growth of good bacteria;
the good bacteria get crowded out from the gut
↓
Changes in the internal mucosal barrier of the intestine
↓
Alteration in gut permeability
↓
Toxic and unwanted molecules pass through the gut lining
↓
Also, the pathogenic bacteria and other substances from within the gut begin to enter blood stream (the condition known as leaky gut)
↓
Invokes an immune response from the body system
↓
Inflammation through the gut lining and intestinal wall
↓
Worsening of leaky gut

When the balance in the gut microbiota shifts in the favor of pathogenic bacteria, it leads to the development of various disorders. Examples of such diseases include metabolic syndrome, inflammatory bowel disease (IBD), obesity, asthma, cognitive and behavioural issues. For instance, IBD occurs due to dysfunction in the interactions between microbes (bacteria), the gut lining and the immune system.

So, let's explore the chain of adverse reaction that begins with consuming foods with high sugar and ends with causing lethal metabolic syndrome and cardiovascular risks.

In addition to promoting growth of pathogenic bacteria in the gut, sugars and refined carbohydrates invokes an insulin response from pancreas every time they enter the body system. As we know that sugars are first broken down into glucose, regular intake of foods with high sugars result in hyperglycemia, and thereby, lead to spike in insulin levels, causing hyperinsulinemia.

Increased insulin levels stimulate the production of pro-inflammatory molecules, contributing towards silent inflammation in the gut lining, resulting in leaky gut.

Regular intake of high sugars/trans-fats
↓
Hyperglycemia
↓
Hyperinsulinemia
↓
Increased production of pro-inflammatory molecules
↓
Leaky gut
↓
Inflammation
↓
Insulin resistance
↓
Obesity and more inflammation
↓

Metabolic syndrome
↓
Increased cardiovascular risks

When our bodies are in a constant state of inflammation, our adrenal glands produce cortisol, the body's primary anti-inflammatory hormone. If silent inflammation persists, the body is subjected to chronic elevated levels of cortisol, worsening the insulin resistance and resulting in obesity. Cortisol also signals to suppress the immune system and is known to kill brain cells, contributing to Alzheimer's disease.

Having understood the causative factors resulting in leaky gut and inflammation, let's explore the type of foods and their culprit ingredients that catalyses their development.

ULTRA-PROCESSED FOODS AND GUT HEALTH

Ultra-processed foods contain substances that have been proven to cause inflammation. These ingredients include:

- Extracted sugar and starch,
- Hydrogenated fats/trans-fats or
- Chemicals made in a laboratory (flavour enhancers and food colourings)

Processed food products include canned foods and salted meat products. Primary examples of ultra-processed foods include aerated drinks, packaged fruit cake, snack foods, packaged breads, buns and pastries, fish or chicken nuggets, instant noodles and soups.

TABLE 3

Adverse effects of industrially processed foods on our health

Type of food	Name of the ingredient/food	Harmful effects
Refined sugar and High Fructose Corn Syrup (HFCS)	• Table sugar, candies and cookies • Soft drinks and aerated drinks • Tropical foods like apple, grapes and oranges	• Glucose and fructose invoke inflammatory response • Glucose also invokes an intense insulin response contributing to persistent hyperinsulinemia leading to comorbidity associated with cardiometabolic syndrome (CMS) • Serves as a feed for harmful bacteria (like streptococcus) that infects the throat as well as the gut • Contributes to oxidative stress, leading to Type 2 diabetes
Refined carbohydrates	• White flour, white rice, pastries, sodas, pasta, white bread, sweets, breakfast cereals and sweets	• Break down into glucose fairly quickly, contributing to persistent state of hyperglycemia • Hyperglycemia → hyperinsulinemia → obesity and insulin resistance → CMS

Type of food	Name of the ingredient/food	Harmful effects
Vegetable oils and seed oils	• Refined sunflower oils, soybean oil, rice bran oil and corn oil, cottonseed oil and sesame oil	• Directly responsible for elevating triglyceride levels, contributes to dyslipidemia and significantly elevates the risk of cardiac arrest and other heart diseases • Polyunsaturated fat chains get easily oxidized upon heating while cooking to form toxic compounds that causes stress to cell membranes • Extremely high amount of omega-6 contributes towards inflammation
Trans-fats	• Processed butter and potato chips • Every kind of fast food and popcorn	• Stimulates the production of pro-inflammatory molecules • Lowers the good cholesterol leading to increased risk of cardiac arrest (heart attacks)

Type of food	Name of the ingredient/food	Harmful effects
Processed meat	• Bacon, ham, smoked meat and sausages	• Cooked at high temperature, processed meat forms advanced glycation end products (AGEs) that leads to 'leaky gut' and cause inflammation • Inflammation increases the risk of heart disease and stomach cancer • Also causes a direct inflammatory response from colon cells, contributing to colon cancer
Alcohol	• Whiskey, scotch, brandy, rum, vodka and tequila	• Exhibit inflammatory response in the liver, contributing to fatty liver disease • Promote the growth of bacterial toxins that lead to 'leaky gut'

Please remember

• Not all vegetable oils and seed oils are bad. In fact, flaxseed oil constitutes the most favourable ratio of omega-3 (anti-inflammatory) to omega-6. Olive oil and coconut oil carry large amounts of saturated fats, which remain stable at high temperatures. That's why these oils have been considered the best for cooking purposes.

- Though beer and red wine have shown some benefits in terms of having anti-bacterial and antioxidant properties, drinking the same in large amounts have the same adverse effects as any other alcohol.

Our health begins from our gut, and we must fix the food first before opting for extensive exercise regime or expensive clinical intervention. Healthy food is essential to reduce the inflammation, lower risk of getting cardiovascular disease, cancer and improve our overall well-being. Nutritionists and physicians following functional medicine recommend eating whole foods. These are the foods available in their natural form that are unprocessed without any added sugar, salt or industrial fat. Further, nutritionists recommend avoiding processed and ultra-processed foods and following a diet having high-fat content with less sugar.

4

TAKING CARE OF YOUR GUT: PREBIOTICS

YOUR GUT HOLDS THE KEY TO YOUR HEALTH

Our gut defines, controls and influences every aspect of our health from digestion, food sensitivities, cravings and body weight to cognitive behaviour, mood, energy, hormonal balance, immunity and overall wellness.

So, the question is, 'How can we rejuvenate our gut microbiome?'

The answer is that our gut needs probiotics and probiotics need prebiotics. Probiotics refer to any microorganism that acts beneficially, particularly for its host. In humans, these good bacteria reside in the gut (small and large intestine).

Prebiotics are a group of food and nutrients upon which our gut microbiome acts and breaks them into products that have a range of benefits from aiding in digestion to developing better immunity. Prebiotics modulate the composition and the function of probiotic bacteria by serving as energy sources for them, thus rejuvenating gut microbiota.

There are certain kinds of foods with a blend of several nutrients that serve as prebiotics for the bacteria living in our gut. Let's have a closer look at them.

Foods with Complex Carbohydrates

Some complex carbohydrates are not digested entirely inside the stomach. This happens because of associated high fibre content present in the food. Instead, they travel to the small intestine to provide essential sustenance for your gut bacteria. Further, undigested food heads towards the colon that becomes an important feed for the probiotic bacteria residing there.

Recent research studies have found that fructo-oligosaccharides (FOS), galacto-oligosaccharides (GOS) and inulin are one of the most significant groups that serve as prebiotics.[18] [19] These are found in foods with high fibre content. The fermentation of prebiotics by gut microbiome generates short-chain fatty acids (SCFAs) like lactic acid, butyric acid and propionic acid.

These SCFAs exhibit the following benefits:

- Lactate kills the lesser-friendly bacteria in the gut by causing acidification. This shifts the balance towards probiotic bacteria in terms of numbers that helps promote digestive health.
- Propionate stimulates T_H2 (T-helper 2) cells[20] and

---

[18]Dorna Davani-Davari, Manica Negahdaripour, Iman Karimzadeh, Milad Mohkam, Seyed Jalil Masoumi, Aydin Berenjian, Younes Ghasemi, 'Prebiotics: Definition, Types, Sources, Mechanisms and Clinical Applications', *Foods*, 2019, p. 8, 92.

[19]B. Wilson, and K. Whelan, 'Prebiotic inulin-type fructans and galacto-oligosaccharides: definition, specificity, function, and application in gastrointestinal disorders', *Journal of Gastroenterology and Hepatology*, 32, 2017, p: 64–68.

[20]T-helper cells activate many other white blood cells and facilitate the release of macrophages to fight against pathogens.

macrophages[21] for the better immune response against foreign pathogens. It also affects dendritic cells[22] in the bone marrows.

• Butyrate helps in maintaining the integrity of the gut lining, thereby preventing or even reversing the inflammation. Hence, it helps in preventing and reversing the progression of cardiometabolic syndrome.

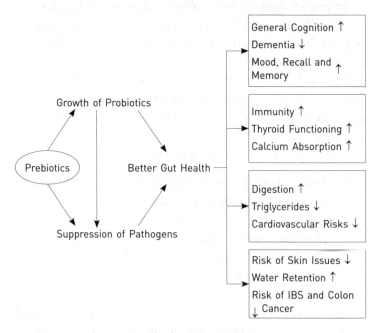

Figure: Prebiotics Effects

---

[21]Macrophages detect and destroy bacteria and other pathogens.
[22]Dendritic cells carry the antigen/foreign pathogen and present it to the fighter cells (like T cells, macrophages) to have them eliminated from the body.

LET FOOD BE THY MEDICINE

Famous ancient Greek physician Hippocrates, renowned as the father of Western medicine, used to prescribe garlic to treat a range of medical conditions.

MAGIC FOOD SOURCES AS PREBIOTICS

There are certain magic ingredients as a source of prebiotics that you never thought could replenish the beneficial bacteria and balance the composition of the gut microbiome in favour of probiotics. Let's explore these ingredients and food products which include certain vegetables, legumes, fruits, nuts and seeds.

TABLE 4

Foods serving as prebiotics, their fibre content and health benefits

Type of food	Name of the ingredient/ food	Composition (fibre per 100 g)	Benefits
Vegetables	Garlic	Fibre: 2.1 g Vitamins B6, C	• Removes heavy metal toxicity • Anti-inflammatory: lowers the risk of cardiac arrests and strokes • Boosts immune system in fighting against cold and flu • Reverses oxidative damage, reducing risk of hypertension, cancer, Alzheimer's and dementia

Type of food	Name of the ingredient/ food	Composition (fibre per 100 g)	Benefits
	Onions	Fibre: 2 g Vitamins C, B6	• Rich in antioxidants: prevents risk of cancer • Lower triglycerides, reduces cholesterol levels • Anti-inflammatory: reduce high blood pressure and prevent blood clots • Improve bone density
	Gingers	Fibre: 14 g Iron, Vitamin B6 and Calcium	• Anti-inflammatory and antispasmodic properties (relieving spasm of involuntary muscles) • Treat the symptoms of nausea and motion sickness • Treat gastrointestinal issues like diarrhoea and constipation • Serve as a potent anti-viral, help in treatment of cold and flu
	Cabbages	Fibre: 2.5 g Vitamins K, C	• Contain more essential and healthy fatty acids (omega-3) per calorie than salmon fish • Manage and regulate blood sugar levels • Boost immune system to prevent cold and flu • High in fibre, effective in cleansing colon
	Broccoli	Fibre: 3 g Vitamins K, C	• Help in preventing as well as treating arthritis • Contain antioxidants, which boost immunity and prevent cancer • Anti-inflammatory in nature
Legumes	Chickpeas	Fibre: 10 g	• Improve metabolism • Manage appetite and help in weight loss • Have low GL that helps in managing blood glucose levels

Type of food	Name of the ingredient/ food	Composition (fibre per 100 g)	Benefits
	Lentils	Fibre: 7.8 g Iron, Zinc, Phosphorus, Potassium, Copper	• Contain potent anti-inflammatory agents and antioxidant • Aids in neuroprotection, preventing risk of Alzheimer's and dementia • High in fibre, promotes healthy bowel movements
	Chicory	Fibre: 3.75 g Vitamin K	• Aids in digestion, helps in treating constipation • Antioxidant properties
	Red kidney beans and soybeans	Fibre: 15.2 g Rich in protein	• Remove sulfite toxicities • Help many enzymes function effectively • High in fibre, effective in cleansing colon
Fruits	Bananas	Fibre: 3 g Vitamin B6, C	• Improve digestive health • Simple carbohydrates serve as quick source of energy • Contain potassium and antioxidants that reduce the risk of a heart disease
	Custard apple	Fibre: 4 g Vitamin B6	• Contains an antioxidant that helps in maintaining healthy vision • Boosts the production and secretion of serotonin and dopamine in the brain, improving mental health and promoting a sense of feel-good • Contains a lot of antioxidants and anti-inflammatory molecules that help in improving insulin resistance and regulates blood pressure

Type of food	Name of the ingredient/ food	Composition (fibre per 100 g)	Benefits
	Kiwi	Fibre: 3 g Vitamin C	• High concentration of Vitamin C and antioxidants help boost the immunity and treat asthma • Helps reduce blood sugar levels and blood pressure • High in fibre and contains enzyme that break down protein and aid in digestion
	Avocado	Fibre: 7 g, Good fat: 12 g Vitamin K	• Healthy fatty acids reduce inflammation • Promotes healthy development of stem cells, reducing risk of blood cancer • Helps reduce blood sugar levels and blood pressure • Lowers down triglycerides by up to 20 per cent • Avocado oil helps in treating auto-immune conditions
Cereal grains	Wheat bran and oat bran	Fibre: Wheat bran: 25 g Oat bran: 15 g	• Promotes healthy digestion, reduces bloating and helps cleanse colon • Have antioxidants that reduces risk of colon cancer
	Barley	Fibre: 16 g	• Improves digestion • Lowers triglycerides and risk of heart disease • Reduces risk of gallstones
	Oats	Fibre: 15 g Manganese, zinc and iron	• Contains antioxidants that stimulates the production of nitric acid, contributing towards lowering of blood pressure • Soluble fibre regulates LDL cholesterol levels, lowers down blood sugar levels and promotes the growth of probiotic bacteria inside the gut

Type of food	Name of the ingredient/ food	Composition (fibre per 100 g)	Benefits
Nuts and seeds	Almonds	Fibre: 11 g Vitamin E	• Vitamin E and other antioxidants reduces oxidative stress • Vitamin E has also been linked with lowering the risk of heart diseases as well as Alzheimer's • Control blood sugar and blood pressure
	Pistachio nuts	Fibre: 10 g Fat: 39 g Vitamin B6	• Contain antioxidants that prevent macular degeneration (which causes blurred vision) and improve vision • High ratio of essential amino acid, responsible for healthy growth of cells and tissues • Stimulate production of nitric acid that helps in regulating blood pressure • Regulate appetite, promote weight loss
	Flaxseeds	Fibre: 28 g Fat: 4.3 g	• Anti-inflammatory: contains more omega-3 (healthy fatty acid) per ounce than the recommended daily amount • Regulate blood sugar and cholesterol levels • High in fibre, serving as a feed for probiotic bacteria, promoting digestive health

While including foods that are mentioned above in the table, a few things must be taken into account:

- The daily limit of fibre content is assumed to be 25 g due to its association with carbohydrates consisting of sugar molecules invoking an insulin response.
- Keep in mind that the portion size of every food varies

in size and weight. The table above has normalized the nutrition value per 100 g, but actual quantity of an ingredient consumed in a meal could vary from just 3 g (in garlic) to 500 g (in cabbage).

- Raw/improperly cooked kidney beans have some toxic proteins and anti-nutrients that can cause vomiting and malabsorption of other nutrients, respectively. So always cook red kidney beans and other beans properly.

- Having a high content of simple carbohydrates per 100 g, a banana should be consumed in a limit, not more than twice a week. So, you can opt for eating slightly unripe banana to gain more out of it without intake of too much sugar.

- Wheat bran contains gluten; avoid eating wheat bran if you have coeliac disease as it is an autoimmune disease that mistakenly targets gluten as a foreign threat to the body causing trouble in the digestive system ranging from abdominal pain to vomiting and diarrhoea.

THE GUT, FOOD AND MOOD

Serotonin, also known as the 'feel-good' hormone, influences how happy we feel and contributes to our overall well-being. Low levels of serotonin have been associated with symptoms of depression, feeling upset and low. And it is crucial to know that serotonin is primarily found in the enteric nervous system[23] located in the gastrointestinal tract. Moreover, 90 per cent of serotonin receptors are also located in the gut.

---

[23]Enteric nervous system is the arrangement of neurons and supporting cells throughout the gastrointestinal tract.

Nutritional psychiatry, a relatively new field of study, has been looking into how gut health and diet can positively or negatively affect the mood. It has found that a healthy diet, rich in prebiotics, improves serotonin levels by stimulating the enteric nervous system to secrete more serotonin. Nutritionally rich foods can enhance the effectiveness of antidepressant drugs (particularly SSRI drugs) and reduce the risk of their side effects, the most common of which are gut-related, including nausea and diarrhoea.

DIET AS AN ANTIDEPRESSANT

A diet must exclude all pro-inflammatory products to keep the mood uplifted and prevent mental fatigue. The best example is the Mediterranean diet, including fishes, eggs, berries, olive oil, cheese, greek yogurt, seafood, and vegetables like cabbage, potatoes and tomatoes. The diet is pretty efficient in controlling symptoms related to anxiety and depression.

In fact, some studies have shown that the right kind of food can not only prevent but also treat mild to moderate levels of depression.[24] [25] These foods include oysters, mussels, salmon, cabbage, broccoli, spinach, lettuce and strawberries. No surprise that these foods are rich in fat and prebiotics and low in sugars.

In the context of depression and other mood problems, a healthy diet can definitely help, but it's only one part of

[24]H. M. Francis, R.J. Stevenson, J. R. Chambers, D. Gupta, B. Newey, C. K. Lim, 'A Brief Diet Intervention Can Reduce Symptoms of Depression in Young Adults—A Randomised Controlled Trial', *PLoS One*, 14(10), 2019.
[25]Sarah Khan and Rafeeq Khan, 'Healthy Diet a Tool to Reduce Anxiety and Depression', *Journal of Depression and Anxiety*, 05, 2016.

treatment. It is virtually impossible to eat your way out of depression or anxiety. You should always seek psychiatric consultancy and treatment in case of moderate to severe depression and contact your doctor if you have been having thoughts of suicide or causing self-harm.

Keeping all the benefits of prebiotics in mind, you should not forget that almost every kind of prebiotic food is available in the form of complex carbohydrates with associated dietary fibre. Large amounts of complex carbohydrates will invoke a prolonged insulin response from the pancreas. Therefore, you should consume prebiotics in a limit such that you do not exceed the carbohydrate intake of 40 g per day. Ideally, it needs to be less than 25 g a day. Hence, you should have your attention focused on a diet with high fat, moderate protein and low carbohydrate.

COMMON FOOD SOURCES OF OMEGA-3 AND OMEGA-6

There's no reason why omega-3 and omega-6 should be only associated with fish oil.

The human body can synthesize all the fatty acids it needs, except for two, known as omega-3 and omega-6. Therefore, they need to be consumed through diet. These essential fatty acids contribute towards

- Improving cardiac health, preventing risk of heart attack
- Uplifting mental health by significantly treating the symptoms of low mood and depression
- Supporting weight loss and promoting bone health
- Treating inflammation and decreasing liver fat, critical in treating fatty liver

- Diminishing the risk of dementia and Alzheimer's
- Controlling the symptoms related to asthma and reactive airway disease[26]

For a long period of time, these essential fatty acids were only known to be available in sea foods, particularly fishes. However, dietary research has proven that there are a lot of foods having rich concentration of omega-3 and omega-6 that can be consumed by a vegetarian.

- Cabbage and cauliflower contains more essential and healthy fatty acids (omega-3) per calorie than salmon fish
- In fact, one ounce of flaxseeds (28 g) offers more than recommended daily amount of omega-3 with favorable omega-3 and omega-6 ratio at 4:1
- Other common food sources include mustard oil, walnuts and berries

---

[26]Bronchi in the lung gets inflamed causing shortness of breath, coughing and/or wheezing.

5

TAKING CARE OF YOUR GUT:
PROBIOTICS

While answering 'how can we rejuvenate the gut health', I said that 'our gut needs probiotics and probiotics need prebiotics'.

In the previous chapter, we focused on the latter half of the answer. In this chapter, we will concentrate on the first half of the statement, which is, our gut needs probiotics.

As defined earlier, probiotics refer to a set of microbes acting beneficially, particularly for its host. In humans, these good bacteria reside in the small and large intestine.

Though intake of prebiotics assists in promoting the growth of probiotics, another healthy alternative is to feed our gut directly with lots of probiotic bacteria. Subsequently, it will remove pathogenic bacteria and maintain gut stability.

Ingestion of probiotics causes vital improvements in balancing intestinal permeability and barrier function, thus treating and reversing the 'leaky gut' syndrome.

FERMENTED PRODUCTS AS THE SOURCE OF PROBIOTICS

Fermented food products are home to probiotic bacteria. Technically speaking, fermentation is an anaerobic process where microbes like bacteria and yeast feed upon carbohydrates (sugar and starch) and break them into alcohol-based products and organic acids. These alcohol-based products need not necessarily mean liquor.

Fermented foods and beverages are made with the help of controlled microbial growth. The phrase 'controlled microbial growth' is of significance as this ensures a large-enough concentration of probiotic bacteria/yeast in the food.

Final biomolecular products like organic acids and alcohols give fermented foods their unique aroma, desirable taste, texture and appearance as well as confer them with a wide range of health benefits.

Though not limited to just these, the key health benefits of fermented foods are as follows:

- **Proper digestion and better cleansing of the colon:** A high concentration of probiotics and the production of certain organic acids through fermentation assist the stomach in digesting food more effectively. Additionally, they allow the entire undigested food to pass through the small intestine smoothly to have it collected by the colon.
- **Enhancement of emotional well-being:** Ingredients like ginger, garlic, lemongrass, cabbage, etc., that are used in making pickle, kimchi and other fermented products reduce stress and anxiety and promote overall emotional well-being.
- **More gut stability, helps remove heavy metal toxicity:** High probiotic content of fermented foods protects the intestinal barrier that inhibits the absorption of heavy metals inducing toxicity, such as lead, arsenic and cadmium.
- **Reduction of cardiovascular risks like hypertension and dyslipidemia:** Numerous prebiotic ingredients are

used while making fermented products. Ingredients like garlic, ginger, onions, mustard seeds, etc., have direct effect on regulating the blood pressure level and lowering triglycerides.

- **Better immunity due to anti-inflammatory, anti-bacterial and anti-viral properties:** Ingredients like turmeric, onions, ginger, garlic and other herbs like kaffir (lime leaves), etc., have anti-inflammatory properties and also help fight against various bacteria as well as viruses.

- **Reduction in risks of cancer:** Whole or raw/unripe ingredients used in many fermented foods are potent antioxidants that prevent and reverse the progression of tumour cell, thus reducing the risk of cancer.

- **Improvement in cognition and brain functionality:** Substances from fermented foods stimulate:
  ○ The production of bioactive peptides[27] exhibiting neuroprotective effects
  ○ The secretion of Brain Derived Neurotrophic Factor BDNF, which serves as a beneficial neurotransmitter essential for learning, comprehension and memory

- **Rich source of multi-vitamins and other micronutrients:** All the additive and core ingredients used for making fermented foods serve as a rich source of a range of vitamins and other micronutrients like potassium, sodium, iron, etc.

Primary examples of fermented foods and beverages include yogurt, pickles, bread, kefir, beers and wines. However, instead of buying industrially made fermented food products, you can make these foods by yourself at home.

---

[27]Small protein molecules that exert a beneficial effect on multiple body functions, positively impacting human health.

IT'S IN OUR TRADITION

Traditionally, Indians have been preparing fermented food products for ages, for example, hung-curd, pickles, fermented raw papaya and buttermilk (chaas), etc. These products have served as rich sources of probiotics. We have been consuming these products regularly as part of our meals. However, as we stepped up in the modern age of globalization and commercialization, we have lost touch with the core cuisine, which was once an integral part of our kitchen and food culture.

With all scientific researches iterating towards the importance of promoting gut health, it is high time that we reintroduce home-made fermented foods in our diet. The practice of fermenting foods is affordable and simplistic. All you need is a few ingredients.

While preparing fermented foods at home, you can save a lot of money and also add unique flavours and interesting textures to your diet. Vegetables such as beetroot, radish, cabbage, carrots and turnips are the easiest foods to ferment at home, as the bacteria living on the surface of these vegetables perform the fermenting for you.

So, let's explore these foods one by one and see how we can ferment them at home.

1. Mango-ginger-garlic pickle

Ingredients

- 2 green mangoes
- 10 garlic cloves
- ¾ cup of sesame oil
- ½ teaspoon each of mustard seeds and cumin seeds (jeera)

- 2 teaspoons of ginger garlic paste (preferably home-made)
- ¼ teaspoon each of turmeric powder and mustard powder
- ¼ each of cumin powder and fenugreek (methi) powder
- 1 teaspoon of red chilli powder
- Salt to taste (put a little extra if the pickle needs to be stored for more than four months)

Method

i.   Cut the raw mangoes into small pieces (the size of half a lemon).
ii. Heat some sesame oil in a pan and add mustard seeds and cumin seeds. Switch off the flame as soon as oil starts to splatter. Keep it aside for some time.
iii. When the oil becomes lukewarm, add all the other ingredients keeping green mango and salt for the end. Mix the ingredients properly for the next couple of minutes.
iv. Transfer the mixture into a jar and keep it aside for three to four days.

Additional benefits

- Raw mango serves as a rich source of antioxidants, helps in reducing cancer risk
- Prevents heat stroke in summers
- Treats liver disease

2. Vegetable pickle

Ingredients

- Any colourful vegetable(s): slices of carrots, red onions, cabbage, radish or turnip

- Flavourings: whole spices, cinnamon, ginger, garlic herbs, lemongrass and kaffir lime leaves
- Vinegar mix: white vinegar, cider, water and sugar (optional)

Method

i.   Cut vegetables into bite-sized pieces. Pack them tightly into clean and dry jars.
ii. Select the flavouring ingredients and add them into the jars of packed vegetables.
iii. Prepare the vinegar mix (equal amount of vinegar, cider and water). Add 1 teaspoon of sugar for each cup of vinegar.
iv. Pour over the vinegar mix upon vegetables until completely soaked.
v.   Close the lid of the jar tightly.
vi. Store in a cool and dark place.
vii. Wait for two to three days for the pickle to turn soft and stronger in flavour.

3. Kaanji

Ingredients

- 2–3 red/black carrots
- 1 large beetroot
- 1–3 mustard seeds powder
- 6–7 cups water

Method

i.   Wash and cut the beetroot and carrots into 2-inch long and about half-inch thick pieces. It is preferred if you keep the outer layer of the carrot intact as it has natural yeast on the surface.

ii.   Put the sliced vegetables in a jar, add mustard powder and salt to it.

iii. Add water and cover the jar with a muslin cloth tied to it.

iv.   Keep the jar outside in sunlight for four to five days for proper fermentation, stirring with a wooden spoon daily.

v.   The kaanji will develop a tangy flavour once it is fermented. Strain the drink and keep it in a refrigerator to enjoy later. Meanwhile, eat the pickle of fermented carrot and beet.

4. Yogurt

A thick and creamy dairy product made from fermenting milk.

Ingredients

- 1–1.5 l of whole or skimmed milk
- ½ cup of yogurt from market. Once you've prepared the yogurt at home, you can save a half cup to use it in the next batch.

Method

i.   Heat the milk right to its boiling temperature. Then allow it to cool.

ii.   When the milk has turned lukewarm, transfer it into a vessel which has an air-tight cover.

iii. Take ½ a cup of milk and add yogurt. Keep whisking the solution smoothly until yogurt is dissolved in the milk.

iv.   Now, pour the thinned yogurt into the warm milk, inoculating the milk with the yogurt culture.

v.   Close the lid. Keep the vessel in a safe place and do not stir the yogurt or move the vessel afterwards. Let the yogurt settle in overnight and enjoy it the next day.

5. Hung curd

Hung curd is basically yogurt without its whey (water) content.

Recipe

- Take a muslin cloth and pour the home-made yogurt on to the cloth.
- Make a closed fold out of the cloth and tie it tightly.
- Hang the cloth in freely suspended form and let the water drain off to turn it into a thick and creamy textured curd.

6. Buttermilk (chaas)

A refreshment drink made from mixing curd or yogurt with cold water.

Ingredients

- 1 cup of yogurt or plain curd
- 2 glasses of water
- A slice of ginger
- 1 teaspoon of finely chopped coriander leaves
- ½ teaspoon of cumin powder
- ½ tsp of black salt
- Table salt (to taste)
- Mint leaves (for garnishing)

Method

i.   Add all the ingredients to a blender.
ii. Blend the mixture till the ingredients are combined properly.
iii. Pour the mixture into a glass and garnish it with fresh mint. Enjoy the drink!

7. Fermented raw papaya

Ingredients

*   1 unripe papaya (½ kg approx.)
*   1 teaspoon non-iodized salt
*   1 kaffir lime leaf (or juice and zest of 1 lime)
*   ½ crushed red chilli or any hot pepper of your choice

Method

i.   Peel the papaya, cut in half and remove its seeds.
ii. You can grate the papaya or cut it into thin slices.
iii. Add salt to the sliced papaya and squeeze the mix to extract its liquid for creating brine with the liquid that comes out of it.
iv. Stir in the chilli and kaffir lime leaf or lime juice.
v.   Pack the mixture into a large and broad container. Add fermentation weight to force the papaya to immerse into its brine completely. You can do this by placing a relatively small bowl into the larger container that can force the papaya down into its brine.
vi. Close the lid and leave the food to ferment at room temperature, away from direct sunlight for one to two weeks.

8. Apple cider vinegar

It is a probiotic additive that can be used while cooking various dishes.

Ingredients

- 2 cups of apple chunks, peels and cores
- 1 teaspoon of raw honey
- 3 cups of filtered water
- 1 cup of apple cider vinegar from market or from previous batch. This is optional to catalyse the fermentation process.

Method

i.   Put the pieces of apple in a glass jar and fill the jar with filtered water.
ii.   Add raw honey to the mixture and shake until it dissolves.
iii. Optional: Add 1 cup of apple cider vinegar to the mixture.
iv.   Cover the jar with muslin cloth tied to it.
v.   Keep the jar still in a dark place for about three to four weeks, occasionally stirring the mixture. Ensure that the apple pieces are submerged.
vi.   After three to four weeks, strain out the apple pieces and compost.
vii. Leave the liquid in the jar for another three to four weeks before using it.

Additional benefits

It is one of the rare foods known to break down and dissolve kidney stones.

9. Tempeh

A traditional probiotic food of Indonesian origin made from fermenting soybeans.

Ingredients

- ½ organic soybeans
- ¾ cup of apple cider vinegar
- 1 teaspoon of tempeh starter (rhizopus mould)

Method

i.   Soak soybeans overnight in water.
ii. Drain the water the next day. This water can be used for the plants outside (not to be used for indoor plants).
iii. Rinse the soybeans smoothly three to four times with clean water.
iv. Put the soybeans in a large pot and pour enough water in it to completely immerse the soybeans. Ideally, the water level should be an inch above soybeans.
v.   Start cooking the soybeans keeping them on high flame. If water starts boiling and starts flowing outside the pot, adjust the flame.
vi. Keep checking the water levels after 10 minutes. You will definitely have to add water three to four times again to to allow soybeans to cook properly. It will take 30–60 minutes to cook.
vii. Cook the beans until they are 80 per cent done, implying that they should be soft but not mushy.
viii. Add vinegar in the end. Mix it properly in soybeans. Drain the water.
ix. Keep heating the soybeans on mild flame to evaporate

any leftover water.

x. Add rhizopus mould (tempeh starter) to catalyze the fermentation. Google to search the nearest location from where you can buy tempeh starter.

xi. Sprinkle 1 teaspoon of the tempeh starter on soybeans and mix it well inside the pot.

xii. Take a reusable Ziploc bag and make pores in it using a wooden toothpick.

xiii. Pour the soybeans into the reusable Ziploc bag. Close the bag tightly.

xiv. Put some weight over the mould and keep the mould in a cold and dry place for 12 hours. Ideally, you can keep it in an oven with its light on. Do not switch on the oven.

xv. Take out the mould from the bag and cut them into small slices. Your tempeh is ready!

xvi. Cook/fry the tempeh properly using the oil of your choice (preferably olive oil) before consuming it. You can also boil or steam them.

10. Kimchi

A Korean dish made by fermenting cabbage.

Ingredients

- 1 Chinese cabbage, chopped lengthwise into slices of 3 cm each
- ¼ salt water
- 1 teaspoon of sugar
- 4 cloves of garlic, crushed
- 2 teaspoon of finely grated ginger
- 1–5 teaspoon of chilli powder

- ½ radish, sliced
- 4 sliced spring onions

Method

i. Cut the cabbage lengthwise into small 3-cm broad pieces and place it in a large bowl.

ii. Sprinkle the salt over the cabbage and gently massage the vegetable using your hands. Allow the sliced cabbage to sit until it has softened.

iii. Press down into the bowl and cover with water. Cover the bowl with a piece of plastic and put some heavy weight on top of it. Allow the mixture to sit for 30 minutes to two hours.

iv. Then drain the water.

v. Rinse the sliced cabbage under cold water and drain it thoroughly squeezing out any excess liquid.

vi. Make a paste of the sugar, garlic, ginger, chilli powder and 2 teaspoons of water. Meanwhile, keep the cabbage aside.

vii. Squeeze out any remaining water from the cabbage. Mix together the drained cabbage, paste sliced radish and spring onions. Ensure that the cabbage, radish and onions are well coated with the paste.

viii. Transfer the kimchi mixture into a clean plastic container until the brine (the liquid that comes out) covers the vegetables, leaving at least one inch of space at the top.

ix. Close the lid on the container loosely for air to escape during the fermenting process

x. Place the container in a cool and dark place for five to seven days.

xi. Check the food daily. Bubbles will appear while fermenting. Open the lid and press down gently twice a day with a clean spoon to expel the bubbles and release the gases produced. Then close the lid loosely as before. Repeat the procedure twice a day for five to seven days.

xii. Once the bubbling stops, your kimchi is ready!

xiii. Transfer the kimchi to smaller containers with airtight lids and keep it in the refrigerator.

Summary: Action Points for Better Gut Health

Consume whole grains, seeds and legumes having complex carbohydrates and dietary fibre.

- Include prebiotics and probiotics in your meal by adding natural herbs, spices and home-made fermented foods.
- Start using cooking oils that are stable at high temperatures like olive oil and coconut oil. Avoid using refined oils.
- Reduce intake of packed fruit juice. Instead, increase your intake of fresh colourful fruits and vegetables.
- Avoid packaged, processed and ultra-processed foods having unhealthy additives and preservatives, inducing heavy metal toxicity and disrupting the gut stability.
- Avoid eating red meat as much as you can. Instead, eat seafood and lean poultry.

SOME DIETARY HABITS TO REMEMBER

In Part III of the book, we're going to discuss life-changing food ingredients that can serve as a magical remedy to not only prevent but also reverse the progression of various chronic disorders. But before we move ahead, here are some dietary habits that you can inculcate in your life for the best results. These minor changes are as important as a nutritious diet.

1. Switch to whole grain

Whatever grain you decide to use, be it wheat, maize, or millets, please ensure that you purchase the whole grain flour.

2. Drinking water

Keep a gap of at least 20 minutes before and after a meal for drinking water. Drinking water immediately after eating can dilute your essential gastric juices, thus hindering digestion. It pushes the food to pass through the stomach and small intestine undigested and unabsorbed. However, if you feel the urge of drinking water, take small sips and do not exceed half a glass. Furthermore, the water being consumed should not be cold and be kept at room temperature.

3. Hot rice/potatoes vs cold rice/potatoes

Keeping cooked rice and potatoes in the refrigerator for two to three hours to cool down converts their starch into a resilient form, known as resistant starch, which is not easily digested by the stomach. It serves as a complex form of carbohydrate that is extremely beneficial for the gut and keeps blood glucose level on check. On the contrary, hot rice and potatoes have zero resistant starch. Hence, they cause an immediate spike in blood sugars when we eat them right after cooking.

4. Switch your refined table sugar with jaggery powder

Throughout the book, I have not mentioned about giving up or avoiding desserts altogether. After all, a little bit of sweetness is required, both in your diet and life. But make sure to switch your refined table sugar to jaggery powder, which is a natural sweetener and available in an unadulterated form without undergoing any industrial treatment.

5. Do not burn your oil and spices while tempering

Use coconut oil and ghee for tempering as they have a high smoking point,[28] which does not allow the free radicals to form. Heat the oil at high flame but switch it to medium (not low) just before adding spices. The sizzling sound of oil sputtering is indicative of spices releasing their essence in the oil. Stir the spices vigorously for 30 seconds to one minute, after which you can turn off the heat. Overcooking will burn your spices and will leave a bitter taste to the entire dish. The worst part is there is no way of reviving your tadka. Once it's gone, you will have to start over again.

---

[28]The smoke point of oil refers to the temperature at which it stops shimmering and then starts giving out smoke.

PART III

MAGICAL INGREDIENTS

MAGICAL INGREDIENTS YOU DID NOT KNOW ABOUT

By now, I am sure you have clarity over the kind of food products that are bad for our health. Also, you must have recognized benefits offered by certain foods.

The previous segment of the book described various foods and ingredients, which either act as prebiotics or serve as a source of probiotics. We discussed the direct positive effects of the healthy and fresh foods on our gut, which in turn are responsible for

- Boosting immunity
- Developing cognition
- Promoting cardiometabolic health
- Improving digestive health
- Maintaining overall mental health and well-being

So, What Next?

This part of the book will highlight the spectrum of 'magical' ingredients offering a wide range of benefits to our health. These ingredients are those we often overlook in the supermarket. We are referring to these ingredients as 'magical' because they do wonders for our health when consumed regularly, even in moderate amounts.

Get Ready to Change Your Life!

The primary focus of this segment of the book is to present healthier food choices. These ingredients are readily available at a reasonable price. They can be conveniently cooked or consumed as any other vegetable or fruit.

The food and ingredients are divided into a few chapters depending upon the category to which they belong. For example, the category of 'herbs and spices' comprises turmeric, fennel, fenugreek, etc. And the category of 'seeds' includes flaxseeds, pumpkin seeds, chia seeds and so on.

I shall outline simple methods to include the ingredients in your daily diet.

6

HEALTHY FATS

Let's start with breaking the myth about fats. As per human biochemistry, fat does not metabolize into fat. This implies that eating foods with high-fat content would not necessarily increase your body weight or fat percentage. As more research has gone into foods and physiology, scientists and nutritionists have unanimously accepted that natural fats are essential for our body and should be consumed liberally.

In fact, anthropologically speaking, fats are something that mankind thrived on for a few million years before learning about agriculture nearly 23,000 years ago.[29] We were hunters and would eat considerably high-fat animal food. Evolutionarily, our physiology is predisposed to eating foods having high amounts of fat with a moderate quantity of proteins and small amounts of complex carbohydrates.

This chapter discusses the benefits of food products predominantly containing 'good fat' or natural fats, like medium-chain triglycerides, omega-3, omega-6 and fats that are stable for Indian cooking. These foods include desi ghee, avocado, coconut oil, olive oil, hard cheese and plenty more. Apart from offering natural fats, these foods are also loaded

---

[29]Ainit Snir, Dani Nadel, Iris Groman-Yaroslavski, Yoel Melamed, Marcelo Sternberg, Ofer Bar-Yosef and Ehud Weiss, 'The Origin of Cultivation and Proto-Weeds, Long Before Neolithic Farming', *PLOS ONE*, 10 (7), 2015.

with micronutrients for additional health benefits.

One of the benefits of eating foods with high-fat content is that you cannot possibly overeat. Think about how easily you can feel satiated by eating two to three whole boiled eggs compared to eating a regular-sized burger along with French fries and a coke. Nutritional foods with high-fat content and limited carbohydrates form the core of weight loss as well as for reversing inflammation and insulin resistance. Let's take a look at some of these foods that have been overlooked for decades.

1. DESI GHEE

Ghee is clarified butter obtained from the milk of cow or buffalo. Pure desi ghee, as we Indians refer to it, is ghee made from cow's milk. Out of the five ingredients making panchamrit, ghee has been traditionally included in all of our Indian meals from dal and khichdi to halwa and on chapattis.

Ghee is believed to carry one of the most valuable and healthiest fats we consume regularly. It imparts a wide array of benefits, ranging from promoting gut health to treating joint pains.

Ghee has not only been the most treasured food since the time Ayurveda was introduced but has also been a staple ingredient in the entire mainland of India since ages. Unfortunately, under the influence of western and modern lifestyle, we swapped ghee with refined oils, which now dieticians have started acknowledging as a grave mistake.

Essential features and benefits

- Contains medium-chain triglycerides, which is a type of good fat that is directly absorbed by the brain for energy, promoting neuronal health

- Facilitates hormonal balancing and helps maintain high levels of good cholesterol
- Has the highest smoking point among edible fatty oils, implying that it does not produce free radicals upon heat, thereby, protecting cell structure and maintaining cellular integrity
- Contains plenty of omega-3 fatty acids along with Vitamin A, improving cardiac health and vision health
- Offers a moist texture to the food, promoting digestion, assimilation of nutrients and intestinal health
- Serves as a lubricating agent for the joint, inducing better mobility, offering relief from joint pain and treating arthritis
- Carries the same kind of fat, which comprises mucosal lining of the stomach, thereby, aiding significantly in repairing the mucus lining of the stomach
- Can be consumed by people who are lactose intolerant

INTERESTING FACTS ABOUT GHEE

- Experts believe that consuming ghee is one of the reasons why India has fewer cases of dementia or Alzheimer's. It is because people till the previous generation ate plenty of ghee with almost every meal.
- Doctors who practice naturopathy direct their patients to take natural medicinal herbs with ghee for treating various ailments, including constipation, joint pains and heart issues.
- The Western countries have started buying the idea that we, as Indians, have been following for centuries. Many of the food companies like Whole Foods Markets, Inc. have begun promoting clarified butter as one of the healthiest fats across the globe.

Feed yourself with the healthiest fat

You can include the benefits of desi ghee in your daily diet using the following ways:

- Add 1 teaspoon of ghee to a portion of your cooked dry vegetables and stewed pulses when you are about to have a meal. This is how our parents and grandparents used to consume ghee. They would add 1–2 teaspoons of ghee to the gravy of legumes and vegetables that were on their plate.
- Use ghee for tempering or roasting whole or ground spices before adding any food in the wok, substituting it for refined oil.
- Add ½–1 teaspoon of ghee while making scrambled eggs or omelet.
- It can be used for spread on chapattis.
- Use ghee while making flaxseed laddoos (alsi ki pinnia) and halwa.

You can prepare ghee at home and that too in a quantity that will suffice for a month. Doing so, you can be assured about consuming unadulterated ghee and avoid spending extra to purchase a relatively expensive alternative for refined oil.

Recipe for making desi ghee from milk

i.   Boil the milk and allow it to cool for four to five hours, permitting a thick layer of cream (malaai) to develop over the top. Remove this layer and collect it in a large bowl. What's left is skimmed milk that we can use for any purpose.
ii. Keep storing the layered cream for 12–14 days and keep it refrigerated.

iii. Take the collected cream and add double the quantity of water to it. Mix and whip till the froth floats on top.

iv. Separate the froth and heat it on a low flame in a saucepan or wok until the fat separates from clarified ghee. Filter out the latter through the use of a sieve and store it for use.

2. AVOCADO

Avocado is a unique fruit, primarily containing healthy fats and complex carbohydrates, along with a blend of multiple vitamins. The fruit is extremely versatile in use as it can be consumed raw in salads, cooked or grilled. It has a relatively long shelf life and does not turn overripe until five days when kept refrigerated. Once you start noticing the benefits of this green superfood, it is something you cannot get enough of.

Essential features and benefits

- It contains loads of omega-3 and monounsaturated fatty acids, which are beneficial for heart, thereby, improving cardiac functioning and health.
- It carries a high percentage of dietary fibre, promoting digestive and intestinal health.
- It imparts a feeling of satiety and fullness with fewer calories, thereby, supporting weight loss.
- It lowers down the levels of LDL (bad) cholesterol and triglycerides, reducing the risk of heart attacks.
- Rich in potassium, it keeps blood pressure under control; regular consumption of avocado helps in preventing hypertension and reducing associated health risks.
- Blended with multiple vitamins (A, D, E and K), avocado

facilitates effective absorption of antioxidants and assimilation of other nutrients from different food sources.

- Packed with Vitamin A and loads of antioxidants, this green superfood protects the eye against macular degeneration and reduces the risk of developing cataracts and promotes eye health.

INTERESTING FACTS ABOUT AVOCADO

- It offers more potassium and sustainable energy than a banana and offers fewer calories.
- Avocado, along with guava, contains the highest protein content among all fruits per serving of one cup of chopped avocado.
- It also carries the highest percentage of dietary fibre (approximately 7 per cent) by weight among all the fruits.

Relish nutrient-rich avocado in your meals

- Consume it as a raw fruit with a pinch of salt and pepper.
- Make an enticing fruit-veggie salad or soup by stuffing avocados with tomatoes, sprouts, berries, etc.
- Make an avocado spread, apply it over a multi-grain bread or on boiled eggs for a healthy and savoury breakfast.
- Add seasoning on scrambled eggs after the eggs are cooked.
- Use as an additional ingredient in scrambled eggs while they are being prepared; they should be added when the eggs are half-cooked to avoid burning them.
- Prepare a lip-smacking and appetizing guacamole using mashed avocado with diced/chopped onions, tomatoes and coriander leaves, and sprinkle some lime juice, salt

and pepper (of your choice) over it.

- Incorporate them in your meal as a grilled side-dish for a delicious smoky flavour.

3. COCONUT OIL

Coconut is a fruit, which botanically is known as a drupe and not a nut. Over the years, we have found plenty of benefits of coconut from its solid fruit, its water inside, leaves and oil. We'll first explore the qualities of coconut oil, which offer healthy fats in the form of medium-chain triglycerides (MCTs). Coconut oil consists of 42 per cent of lauric acid, which gives coconut oil its characteristic qualities discussed below.

Essential features and benefits

- It is stable at high heat preventing the oil from producing free radicals, protecting cell structure and maintaining cellular integrity.
- Lauric acid offers a wide array of benefits from boosting immunity to promoting gut health. It also helps in aiding weight loss by stimulating the burning of calories and deposited fat.
- Given that lauric acid is a type of MCT, it helps in boosting brain and cognitive function. Hence, it contributes in protection against dementia and Alzheimer's.
- Combination of healthy fatty acids promotes cardiovascular health and improves HDL (good) cholesterol levels.
- It stimulates the production of ketones in the liver, offering sustainable energy throughout the day while controlling the appetite.

INTERESTING FACTS ABOUT COCONUT OIL

- Coconut oil has been used to follow a practice called oil pulling, which includes swishing the oil in your mouth to remove bacteria and promote oral hygiene.
- With its roots originating from Ayurveda, oil pulling 'pulls out' the harmful bacteria from the mouth and removes them from your oral cavity as you spit out the oil while swishing.

Benefits

- Kills and removes harmful bacteria from your mouth
- Prevents bad breath and cavities
- Improves gum health

How to do it?

Start your day with oil pulling even before brushing your teeth:

- Take 1 teaspoon of coconut oil in your mouth and start swishing the oil back and forth in between your teeth for at least 10 minutes. Do not swallow the oil as it can push toxins from your mouth to your gut.
- Spit the oil in the sink and rinse your mouth with warm salt water to remove any of the toxic leftovers.
- Then brush your teeth as you regularly do.

Pour some magic of coconut oil in your meals

- It can be used as a substitute for refined oil in cooking, tempering and/or sautéing in a manner similar to how we use any vegetable oil.
- It can be used as an essential ingredient in making home-made dark chocolate.

- Blend a cup of freshly brewed coffee with 2 teaspoons each of coconut oil and cacao butter for a creamy beverage to kick-start your day with a bulletproof coffee, also called keto coffee.

4. OLIVE OIL

Olive oil is a naturally occurring oil extracted from olives. The oil, having a high smoking point, is suitable for different styles of cooking. In the market, it is available in three forms: refined, virgin and extra-virgin. Ensure that you only purchase the first two.

Essential features and benefits

- It carries oleic acid along with omega-3 and omega-6, which promote cardiac health.
- It is resistant to high heat—its constituents do not break into free radicals upon heating, thus making olive oil a healthy choice for cooking.
- It serves as a source of powerful antioxidants, reducing the risk of cancer and other chronic diseases.
- The oil has strong anti-inflammatory properties owing to oleic acid, reducing the oxidative stress inside a body. This helps in alleviating the symptoms of joint pain and rheumatoid arthritis, further reducing the risk of cancer.
- It protects blood cholesterol from getting oxidized, thereby, helps to lower the risk of heart disease.
- It prevents and reduces the risk of having a stroke.
- It improves insulin sensitivity and has been shown to reduce the risk of Type 2 diabetes by over 40 per cent.

Include much stable and healthier fats in your meal

- Substitute refined oil with olive oil for cooking and sautéing.
- Use olive oil as dressing on fruit or vegetable salads.
- Prepare rich and savoury classical chickpea hummus using olive oil, which is full of flavour and taste.
- It can also be used for oil pulling early in the morning for promoting oral health. Use it in the same manner you would use coconut oil.
- Olive oil is an integral ingredient to be used in preparing Mediterranean food like stewed vegetable and lentil dishes, Greek lemon rice, Greek salad, tabbouleh, etc.

5. FLAXSEED OIL

Flaxseed oil, also identified as linseed oil, is derived from ripened flaxseeds that have been ground and cold-pressed to release their natural oil. Flaxseed oil is packed with healthy fatty acids, proteins and dietary fibre affecting multiple body organs, including muscles, heart, liver, stomach, intestines, etc.

Essential features and benefits

- It comes loaded with omega-3 and omega-6, which assists in promoting cardiac health and supporting weight loss.
- It exhibits potent anti-inflammatory properties, reducing liver fat, which facilitates reversal of the progression of non-alcoholic fatty liver disease (NAFLD).
- It works as a laxative if consumed regularly and helps in treating constipation and alleviates symptoms of irritable bowel syndrome (IBS).

- It includes antioxidant agents, thereby, preventing the risk of cancer.
- It comes packed with proteins, promoting bone health.
- It also improves overall metabolism of the body.

INTERESTING FACTS ABOUT FLAXSEED OIL

- Flaxseed oil offers about 7 g omega-3 per tablespoon, which makes it by far the richest source of this heart-healthy fatty acid, exceeding its recommended daily intake.
- The oil also contains the second most favourable ratio of omega-3 to omega-6 after ghee at ratio of 4:1, implying that omega-3 content is four times higher than that of omega-6, which is what dieticians prefer and recommend.

Mix the goodness of healthy fats with flaxseed oil

- Use it for salad dressing.
- Incorporate the oil making purees and sauces from herbs and spices.
- Add 1 tablespoon of flaxseed oil in smoothies and shakes.

Caution: Do not use flaxseed oil for cooking as it has a low smoking point and forms free radicals at high temperatures causing harm to the body.

6. CASTOR OIL

Castor oil is a multi-purpose vegetable oil obtained from seeds of a plant, which is native to tropical areas of Africa and Asia. The oil is used to treat a range of medical conditions, specifically those pertaining to digestion and skin.

Essential features and benefits

- It serves as a potent laxative and is extremely effective in treating constipation.
- It boosts the immune system and improves blood circulation.

How to consume

- Use it as an additive (1 tbsp) while your dal or vegetable is being cooked.

Caution: Castor oil can induce labor, because of which medical professionals use it to induce childbirth when a pregnant woman is having specific issues during delivery. It's the reason why women at all stages of pregnancy should avoid consuming castor oil. Never give castor oil to a pregnant woman to help her induce labor without consulting a gynaecologist.

7. DARK CHOCOLATE

We often associate chocolate with something sweet. However, the fact is that chocolate, in its naturally occurring form, tastes extremely bitter. The bittersweet dark chocolate is the one that comes closest to its natural disposition, comprising a high percentage of cacao solids (65–80 per cent), cacao butter and very little sugar, without any milk.

Essential features and benefits

- Derived from cacao beans, which are rich in antioxidants (probably the best source), dark chocolate helps prevent DNA damage, thereby, reducing the risk of cancer.

- It helps stimulate the production of nitric oxide that helps in regulating blood pressure.
- Containing oleic acid, it is a kind of a healthy fat that is also found in olive oil, which is regarded as beneficial for cardiac health.
- It exhibits anti-inflammatory properties, reducing the risk of stroke and other cardiovascular disorders.
- It raises levels of good cholesterol and reduces the risk of diabetes by improving insulin sensitivity.
- It is extremely rich in iron, magnesium, copper and manganese.

INTERESTING FACTS ABOUT CHOCOLATE

The term chocolate can be traced back to the Aztec word 'xocoatl', which was referred to as a bitter drink brewed from cacao beans.

100 g of dark chocolate contains 600 calories with a little to moderate amount of sugar. Therefore, it should be consumed with caution.

Chocolates we think we're having

Chocolate is available in solid, paste or liquid state and is made from roasting and grounding cacao seeds. Typically, chocolate is sweetened to make it more palatable. A product should contain at least 35 per cent of purest chocolate, derived from cacao beans, to serve its benefits. Healthiest of all of such products are the ones having at least 70 per cent of pure chocolate. The more, the better! So, consume dark chocolates having about 35-70 per cent of pure chocolate in mild-to-moderate amount once to twice a week.

The chocolates commonly available in the market do not even include 10 per cent of cacao extract, which is why some brands would not label their product as chocolate. The so-called white chocolates do not contain the extract of cacao beans. These are called chocolates only because they incorporate cacao butter. But technically, they are just candies with milk solids and a lot of sugar.

These types of sweetened chocolates do not provide any of the said benefits they claim to have. Instead, a large amount of sugar consumed with them serves as a feed for harmful bacteria inside the gut, causing inflammation and enhancing the risk of diabetes.

Say yes to the bittersweet

Prepare dark chocolate at home or buy one of a genuine and reputed brand from the market and consume it in small amounts as a dessert after a meal.

8. DAHI (YOGURT)

Yogurt is a thick and creamy dairy product made from fermenting milk. Fermentation breaks the sugar present in the form of lactose into beneficial alcohol-based products and organic acids.

Essential features and benefits

- It contains a hearty dose of probiotics, shifting the balance towards good bacteria in our gut.
- It helps in digestion and promotes good intestinal health.

- It is proven to offer relief in alleviating symptoms of IBS syndrome.
- A rich source of protein and calcium, it helps in building muscular strength and protects against osteoporosis.
- It helps in relaxing the muscular stress, helping in faster post-workout recovery.
- It serves as an excellent alternative for people having lactose intolerance who cannot drink milk.
- It facilitates functioning of the active T-cells, enhancing immunity.

Following our tradition: Why it is best to prepare yogurt at home

Yogurt, traditionally referred to as dahi in the Indian mainland, has been an integral part of every staple diet of different regions across India. It is said that the entire Indian cuisine can collapse if we remove yogurt from it.

The entire nation consumes yogurt in one form or the other. North Indians consume it with dry vegetables, paranthe and in the form of shrikhand, lassi, or chaas. On the other hand, South Indians relish curd-rice or curd by itself.

Ancient Indian texts, dating back to pre-historic times, have made reference to the consumption of fermented milk. Moreover, there is a mention of a curd rice dish in the Rig Veda. And since those times, our ancestors have been making yogurt by themselves. Little did they know about the bacteria inside it, but they knew it helped improve digestion and promote overall gut health.

Now, with the progression of science, we have unfolded the mysteries of homemade yogurt, which contains both probiotics and prebiotics. But as we have discovered and explained the benefits of it, we have forgotten how our mothers prepared yogurt at home. Our mothers used to prepare it by fermenting half a litre or a litre of milk with one to 2 teaspoons of yogurt saved from the previous batch.

Nowadays, only a few of us bother to make dahi at home. Instead, we buy the pasteurized version from shops at inflated prices, not realizing that it has zero medicinal effects. It is because pasteurization involves heating the milk at very high temperatures. Such extreme temperature not only kills the harmful bacteria but also destroys the beneficial ones.

We have come to a point where food companies are trying to sell natural bacteria-filled yogurt to us at much higher rates because they know that we have turned our backs on our own traditions. So, do yourself a favour: follow the old Indian tradition of making dahi at home. Eventually, you will end up eating quality Indian dahi that will keep you healthy.

Smoothen your meal with thick and creamy yogurt

- Consume it raw as prepared at home.
- It can be taken as a complimentary dish with our main meals.
- Add roasted cumin seed powder and salt to the yogurt and consume it as an instant remedy to treat indigestion.
- Pour it over a bowl of fruit and/or vegetable salad.
- Yogurt can also be added to your oatmeal, along with berries, dry fruits and nuts to make for a healthy breakfast option.

9. WHOLE MILK

Whole milk is what we purchase directly from a cattle farmer. We do so because this milk (of a cow or buffalo) contains healthy fat content that is otherwise removed from skimmed and toned milk processed in the industries. It contains all the nutrients needed for a calf. It is no surprise that the very nutrients offer similar health benefits to humans too.

Essential features and benefits

- It promotes bone health and helps prevent osteoporosis in elderly.
- It is an excellent source of protein, calcium, phosphorus, multiple vitamins, and helps develop strong bones and muscular strength.
- It helps boost immunity.

Add to the shelf life

- Do not boil whole milk to the degree that it overflows from the pan. The high temperature denatures the protein and destroys vitamins. Heat it till it starts sputtering. Hold the flame to about half a minute and then turn it off. You need not keep the milk out in the open and can refrigerate it immediately.

Caution: Many people have inborn lactose intolerance. They should avoid drinking milk.

Include wholesome goodness of milk in your diet

- Drink a glass of milk once or twice a day.
- Add it in traditional desserts, smoothies, shakes and refreshment drinks.
- Pour some milk in your cereal-based snacks or oatmeal.

- You can pour some in your coffee too, but in low quantity.

10. HARD CHEESE

Not every type of cheese is equally healthy. Hard cheese, what we are referring to, is the natural cheese produced from coagulating milk either using an acidic ingredient like lemon or bio-enzymes called rennet.

On the other hand, soft cheese is industrially processed cheese with a smooth and creamy texture. It is made from combining natural cheese with milk solids, water, plus stabilizers for extra shelf life, and emulsifying salts, which are unhealthy to consume.

It is recommended to buy non-branded cheese from local dairy shops instead of buying packed cheese from supermarkets.

Essential features and benefits

- Raw cheese aids in digestion.
- It contains plenty of omega-3 fatty acids along with Vitamin A, Vitamin K, Vitamin B-6 and Vitamin B-12. These nutrients play a vital role in improving cardiac, vision and neuronal health. It also helps boost immunity.
- It is an excellent source of protein and calcium, which helps in building muscular strength and promoting bone health.
- Aged hard cheeses like Cheddar, Swiss, and Parmesan contain minute amounts of lactose. Therefore, they are safe to be consumed by people who are lactose intolerant.

Enjoy the cheesy bite!

- Consume finely cut raw cheese with salt and pepper sprinkled over it as a healthy snacking option.
- Grate some Parmesan onto roasted broccoli or cauliflower for a cheesy and crunchy bite!
- Savour the delicious taste of scrambled cheese cooked in olive oil, with added onion, garlic, ginger and green chilli.
- Enjoy making flavourful grilled, barbequed or baked cheese with capsicum.
- Prepare mouthwatering shahi paneer with thick and creamy gravy.
- Use it as an ingredient in making cheese-peas, potato-cheese, or mix-vegetable.

Caution: Do not binge eat cheese as it has been known for causing calcium stones and high blood pressure.

7

HERBS AND SPICES

Culturally, we have been using herbs and spices to add flavour to our meals. Little did we know that they have a lot more to offer than just aroma and taste. Ayurveda, which focuses on healing through lifestyle and food, is replete with information highlighting benefits of various herbs and spices and how to use them for medicinal purposes. Herbs and spices balance the energies manifesting in our bodies in the form of three *doshas*: *vata, pitta* and *kapha* promoting natural healing and overall well-being.

> 'Ounce for ounce, herbs and spices have more antioxidants than any other food group.'
>
> —Michael Greger, MD
> Advocate of a whole-food, plant-based diet

Every herb and spice has a different nature or impact on the human body. Some of them enhance *agni*—the digestive fire—and heal and reduce injury. Others provide a cooling effect to help us relax and sleep. This chapter will pick up one herb or spice at a time. We will be discussing the nutritional profile and health benefits of ginger, garlic, turmeric, coriander, mint and many more. You can use herbs and spices in some of the interesting ways described to prepare lip-smacking curries, chutneys and beverages.

Apart from offering antioxidants and anti-inflammatory benefits, ample evidence suggests that spices and herbs possess anti-carcinogenic and cholesterol-lowering properties. Further, they also help in improving cognition and stabilizing mood. Power-packed with micronutrients, vitamins and other bioactive constituents, herbs and spices offer a diverse range of health benefits.

1. ADRAK (GINGER)

Ginger is a flowering plant whose root we use as a zesty culinary ingredient. It is one of the healthiest spices with a sharp, mildly sweet and a slightly woody flavour. Having a long history of being used in alternate/traditional medicine, this aromatic spice imparts numerous health benefits related to immunity, gastrointestinal and respiratory systems.

Essential features and benefits

- Power-packed with antioxidants and anti-inflammatory components, it helps in reducing the risk of cancer and various chronic illnesses.
- It exhibits anti-microbial attributes, helps in treating symptoms of common cold, flu, sore throat, bronchitis, etc.
- It helps in breaking down mucus, improving the circulation of air inside the body, which is especially beneficial for patients with asthma and chronic obstructive pulmonary disease (COPD).
- It is known to treat nausea, anxiety, symptoms of gastric reflux and morning sickness.

- Alleviating oxidative stress, it helps prevent Alzheimer's and protects against age-related decline in cognitive function.
- Ginger is known to have impressive positive effects in reducing blood sugars and improving symptoms of osteoarthritis.

Savour the lip-smacking flavour with powerful health benefits

- Make a ginger-lemon tea or masala chai
- Add finely chopped ginger in cooked lentil, scrambled eggs and omelettes.
- Include ginger as an ingredient in making purée for gravy of vegetables. The purée may include onions, tomatoes, garlic and/or coriander leaves.
- Using the extract of ginger with honey, make a honey-ginger paste to help relieve sore throat symptoms.
- Spice up your morning by adding ground ginger to your coffee.
- Add ginger juice to your smoothies for a zesty drink.

Relish all the medicinal benefits with ginger ale (non-alcoholic)

Ginger ale is a refreshing anti-inflammatory drink, serving as an elixir for the gut microbiome. It is made using ginger juice, sugar, club soda, by sprinkling some lemon juice and tossing in a few leaves of mint.

Method

i. Grate ginger finely amounting to 2–3 teaspoons and put it in the pan.

ii. Add ¾ cup of sugar and pour 1 cup of water in the pan.

iii. Heat the mixture on medium-high flame for four to five minutes till the sugar dissolves and ginger extract begins to blend in the water.

iv. Switch off the flame, cover the pan and let it rest for one hour.

v. Filter out the ginger residues using a sieve and collect the ginger syrup in a small container.

vi. Keep the container refrigerated and use small amounts of syrup whenever you have to drink the ale.

vii. Now, for making the ale, use 4–5 teaspoons of ginger syrup and add to it 300 ml of cold soda or carbonated water. Sprinkle half a lemon to it and add some ice cubes to make it colder.

viii. Garnish the drink by tossing a couple of fresh mint leaves!

2. LEHSUN (GARLIC)

Garlic is a herb that is closely related to onion, leeks and chives. It is grown around the world and has widely been used since ancient times. Practitioners of traditional medicine have been using garlic since the vedic period in the treatment of cardiovascular ailments, including hypertension, stroke, atherosclerosis, etc.

In fact, Hippocrates, who is hailed as the 'father of medicine', was known to have prescribed garlic for treating various ailments around 400 BC. It was used to combat infection, heal wounds, treat leprosy and ease digestion.

Essential features and benefits

- It enhances immunity and protects against common cold and flu.
- It reduces LDL (bad) cholesterol as well as improves the HDL (good) cholesterol levels, diminishing the risk of heart attack and other heart diseases.
- It also reduces the risk of stroke.
- It subdues daily fatigue and enhances stamina needed for physical activities.
- By regulating blood pressure, it effectively treats hypertension.
- It contains certain antioxidants, which help in preventing dementia and Alzheimer's.
- Sulfur compounds in garlic exhibit chelating properties, effects of which have been scientifically studied. These compounds impart garlic with the capabilities of eliminating heavy metal toxicities and serve as a blood purifier.

Make use of your global condiment

- Garlic is one ingredient that has been used by every culture in their staple food, be it Chinese garlic chicken, Lebanese garlic sauce or Molokhia, which is a traditional dish of Arabs.
- Changing demographics have brought about diversity in Indian cuisine. However, there is one thing which has remained constant in every staple diet among different regions, and that is garlic. It is an essential herb while tempering Punjabi dals and chicken curries and almost every lentil dish falling under Indian cuisines. Further, it also serves as the main ingredient for making Gujarati thepla, Rajasthani dal baati churma, South Indian pondu

(garlic) chutney, rasam, or Bengali fish curry.

- Add finely chopped garlic in scrambled eggs and omelettes.
- Always incorporate garlic along with other spices while tempering for making any kind of curry for vegetables or lentil dishes.
- Grind 10–15 cloves of garlic while making purée for vegetable curries. The purée may include onions, tomatoes, ginger and/or coriander leaves.
- Add chopped garlic as an ingredient in savoury dishes, soups, sauces, etc.

Caution: Do not binge on garlic if you're taking blood thinners as both of them have the same effect.

3. HALDI (TURMERIC)

Turmeric, recognized as one of the most powerful spices, can be easily found in Indian cuisine and household. Turmeric has a slightly bitter taste, which is why it is used in moderate amounts mainly as a coloring agent in curries, mustards and cheeses.

Turmeric has an extremely long history of being used in Indian traditional medicine since the vedic times. It is so integral to our culture that we forced the US Patent and Trademark Office (PTO) to revoke a controversial patent, which was granted in 1995 to researchers in the United States on the use of powdered turmeric for healing wounds.[30]

---

[30]Raj Chengappa, 'Patents: India wins a victory over turmeric but the war is on', *India Today*, 14 May 2013, https://www.indiatoday.in/magazine/science-and-technology/story/19970908-patents-india-wins-a-victory-over-turmeric-but-the-war-is-on-832438-1997-09-08. Accessed on 20 December 2021.

Essential features and benefits

- The main biologically active compound in turmeric is curcumin. It indirectly plays a critical role in protecting a person against depression and Alzheimer's.
- It exhibits potent anti-allergic properties, serving as a remedy for treating allergic cough, sneezing and sinusitis.
- It possesses powerful anti-inflammatory properties that help in imparting relief from the pain associated with rheumatoid arthritis and osteoarthritis.
- It controls one's blood sugar levels, delaying and preventing Type 2 diabetes.
- It enhances immunity, powering our body to fight against common viruses and bacteria, reducing the risk of catching a flu.

Detoxifying what detoxifies us: Promoting liver health

Turmeric is considered to be the most effective spice in promoting liver health. Curcumin in turmeric reduces liver toxicity caused by environmental toxicants such as arsenic, cadmium, chromium, lead and mercury. It regulates glutathione level, enhancing the antioxidant capacity of liver protecting the liver enzymes against oxidative stress.

Add a vibrant color of health to your food

- Use ½–1 teaspoon of turmeric powder while tempering spices in olive oil or ghee before adding the mix into the entire broth of lentil dishes or any other vegetable
- Add ½ teaspoon of whole turmeric powder in a warm glass of whole milk.

- Add it as an ingredient in turmeric-ginger-honey tea.

Give your evening coffee a new twist with turmeric latte (haldi doodh)

1. Combine 1 glass of almond milk, 1 teaspoon of whole turmeric powder, ½ teaspoon of honey, ½ teaspoon of grated ginger and ¼ teaspoon of pepper in a blender.
2. Blend the mix for about a minute to give it a smooth texture.
3. Pour the milk in a small pan and keep over medium-high heat until it starts to sputter. Do not boil it.
4. Transfer the steaming hot milk to a mug, sprinkle some cinnamon over it. Enjoy the drink!

Notes

- Curcumin is poorly absorbed into the bloodstream. Consume black pepper with turmeric to significantly enhance the absorption of curcumin.
- Avoid purchasing packed turmeric powder as much as possible. You can make a fine powder of turmeric pieces using a mixer-grinder machine at home.

4. DHANIYA (CORIANDER/CILANTRO)

Coriander is a herb that comes from the plant, *Coriandrum sativum*, which is closely related to parsley, carrots and celery. Its leaves and seeds are typically used for providing a pleasant aroma to the food and for flavouring ingredients. However, this condiment does a lot more than just impart pleasant taste in our meals.

Essential features and benefits

- It eliminates heavy metal toxicities—one of the very few herbs capable of removing mercury toxicities from the body and decreasing the absorption of excessive lead.
- It exhibits antiviral properties, boosting immunity against influenza and other viruses.
- Packed with antioxidants, it helps prevent inflammation and reverse the progression of cardiometabolic disorders.
- It decreases anxiety and improves memory.
- It helps in lowering down blood pressure and is beneficial for patients with hypertension.
- Coriander seeds can help treat Type 2 diabetes by activating certain enzymes in the body that stimulate insulin production and improve carbohydrate metabolism.

Include coriander for an aromatic experience

- Relish the wholesome goodness of coriander seeds by adding them in your baked goods, roasted vegetables and cooked lentil dishes.
- Soak the seeds overnight and drink a glass full of that first thing in the morning to keep your blood sugar levels under check throughout the day.
- Ground the seeds to make fine dhaniya powder and add them in your home-made garam masala. You may also include it in your dals and vegetable curries.
- Add corinader leaves for garnishing your rice dishes, vegetables, soups and salads.
- Use these leaves in cold pasta, lentils, fresh tomato salsa, or noodle dishes.
- Make a purée of leaves along with garlic, ginger and tomatoes

and use it for making a flavoursome vegetable gravy.
• The ancient Egyptians used to drink coriander tea to treat clinical conditions such as urinary tract infections and headaches.

THE CHELATING EFFECT:
FIGHTING AGAINST HEAVY METAL TOXICITY

As already discussed in the book, heavy metal enters our bloodstream through various channels and bind to the healthy tissues, imparting toxicities, damaging DNA and increasing the risk of developing cancer.

Chelation is a type of a strong bond formed between a chemical substance and a metal. The compounds that form the bond with metals are known as chelating agents.

Garlic, coriander leaves (cilantro) and turmeric have proven to be the most effective herbs in removing heavy metal toxicities, serving as guardians against chronic diseases. These herbs are densely packed with chelating compounds.

Coriander leaves, containing a potent mix of chelating agents, are capable of removing mercury and decreasing the absorption of lead.

Turmeric contains curcumin, which exhibits chelating properties and imparts the liver with enhanced antioxidant capabilities. It facilitates in removing toxicities like arsenic, cadmium, chromium, lead and mercury from the blood with the help of the liver.

Garlic and **asafetida** (hing) contain a blend of multiple bioactive compounds containing sulfur. Sulfur binds to heavy metals and pulls them away from healthy tissues into the bloodstream. As the blood is circulated through kidneys, heavy metals get filtered out in the urine and eliminated from the body.

5. PUDINA (MINT)

Mint is a cooling herb that belongs to the genus *mentha*, plants of which are especially recognized for imparting a refreshing sensation. They are added to foods for flavouring, freshness and aroma. Mint can be used as green leaves or in dried form in a variety of foods and drinks, ranging from hot herbal tea and salads to cool refreshments and desserts.

Essential features and benefits

- Chewing fresh leaves of mint or making a tea from mint leaves can help mask bad breath and also kill the bacteria causing it.
- Packed with menthol, it serves as a remedy for indigestion and chest pains.
- It is loaded with potent antioxidants, protects cells from oxidative stress and prevents inflammation.
- It includes a decent amount of Vitamin A, which is vital for ocular health.

Breathe in the cooling freshness of mint

Because of its biting flavour, mint is hard to consume in large quantities as other herbs. However, you can include it in small amounts regularly in different meals of the day.

- Add mint in herbal tea, along with ginger and other spices.
- Garnish your cooked dry vegetables and rice with mint.
- Include it in salads, smoothies and desserts.
- Toss a leaf or two in your lemon drink or other refreshing beverages.

Make your own mint chutney

1. Pluck mint leaves from their stems. Collect them filling up to 2 cups. Rinse them properly with water and put them in the grinder machine.
2. Combine them with finely chopped ginger (a piece of 1 inch) and two pieces of green chilies.
3. Add salt to taste and ¼ teaspoon each of dry mango powder, roasted cumin powder and black salt.
4. Add ½ teaspoon of lime juice to increase the shelf life and prevent the chutney from discoloration.
5. Pour 1–2 teaspooon of water in the mix and grind it well to a smooth consistency. Do not add too much water.
6. Serve the chutney immediately with evening snacks or traditional meals, or refrigerate it for later use. It will remain good for four to five days when refrigerated.

FASCINATING USAGE AND BENEFITS OF PEPPERMINT OIL

Peppermint is a special hybrid variety of mint, formed after making a cross between watermint and spearmint. There has been more than a sufficient number of studies to confirm that inhaling the aroma of peppermint oil exhibits positive effects on brain functioning.[31] [32]

---

[31] Mark Moss, Steven Hewitt, Lucy Moss, Keith Wesnes, 'Modulation of Cognitive Performance and Mood by Aromas of Peppermint and Ylang-Ylang', *Int J. Neurosci*, January 2008; 118(1), p: 59–77.

[32] B. Deivanayagame, A. V. Siva Kumar, K.N. Maruthy, S.K. Kareem, 'Effect of Peppermint Aroma on Short Term Memory and Cognition in Healthy Volunteers' 8, 2020, p: 16–20.

It has been shown to

- Improve memory
- Increase alertness
- Decrease levels of frustration, anxiety and fatigue
- Help relieve symptoms of IBS

6. KARIPATTA (CURRY LEAVES)

Curry leaves are the foliage of the curry tree, *Murraya koenigii*, which is native to India. These leaves are used for culinary as well as medicinal applications. Highly aromatic and unique in flavour, they offer a plethora of health benefits from being anti-inflammatory to imparting neuroprotective effects.

Essential features and benefits

- It acts as a powerful punch of antioxidants reducing the risk of cancer, preventing and reversing the progression of chronic cardiometabolic disorders.
- It helps fight inflammation and lowers cholesterol levels, diminishing the risk of heart diseases.
- It serves as a remedy for controlling blood sugar levels.
- A few studies have noted neuroprotective effects of certain compounds in curry leaves that can sharpen the memory and protect against dementia and Alzheimer's.[33] [34]

---

[33]Rupali Patil, Kiran Dhawale, Hanmant Gound and Rajendra Gadakh, 'Protective Effect of Leaves of Murraya koenigii on Reserpine-Induced Orofacial Dyskinesia', *Iranian Journal of Pharmaceutical Research*, 2012, p: 635–41.

[34]Mani Vasudevan and Milind Parle, 'Antiamnesic potential of Murraya

- Though not known for their role in weight control, curry leaves carry a specific type of alkaloid that acts as an antagonist to mass gain, aiding in weight loss.
- As strange as it may sound, curry leaves can help in combating both diarrhoea and constipation.
- Rich in Vitamin A, they help in preventing the development of cataracts.

Experience the eccentric flavour of curry leaves

- Use them in traditional Indian curries of Punjabi, Rajasthani, Bengali or South Indian cuisine.
- Toss them in traditional South Indian recipe called sambhar.
- Add them in the gravy of freshly cooked lentils.
- Sauté curry leaves in ghee on high flame and then add the softened leaves to any dish of your liking.

DID YOU KNOW?

- South Indian cuisine boasts of curry leaves as its one constant ingredient in various foods. For example, curry leaves are included as the main condiment in preparing chutneys and dhokla in Gujarat, poha in Maharashtra, traditional Hyderabadi biryani in Andhra Pradesh, Poriyal in Kerala and of course, every South Indian curry.
- Dried curry leaves are readily available in grocery stores. They might also be found in abundance in the park or garden nearby you. You can collect them from there if you can recognize them.

Growing your own herbs

Mint, cilantro and curry leaves are the herbs that are the easiest to grow in small pots in your balcony. These herbs do not require the addition of fertilizers. The amount of sunlight that brightens up your balcony is enough for these plants to grow. Also, they do not require water in excess. Watering them once a day will do. In short, these herbs do not require constant attention for their growth.

For growing herbs, you need seeds of coriander and stems of curry leaves and mint with their leaves intact. The most essential point to consider is to sow the seeds and stems in early winters when the temperature is in the range of 15–25 degrees Celsius.

1. Soak coriander seeds for 24 hours before they turn into seedlings.
2. Take 3 small pots or containers, one for each condiment. Make small holes at the side of the pots or bottom of the containers to drain extra water.
3. Fill in the pots with a mixture of garden soil, vermicompost and cocopeat in an approximate ratio of 2:2:1.
4. Plant the stems of mint and curry leaves such that they are embedded in the soil for about an inch. The part of the stem planted in the soil should be clear off any leaves or their petiole residues.
5. Also, sow 1 teaspoon coriander seeds about half to one inch deep in the soil. Place the seeds two inches apart from each other and press the soil over them.
6. These herbs will grow and be ready for use in the next six weeks.

Why grow your own herbs?

Herbs like mint, cilantro and curry leaves are usually not tempered or sautéed on high flame. They are either added at last or used for garnishing a dish. So, all we do is wash them properly before adding them to our foods. This does not kill the harmful bacteria in herbs, if any. Moreover, growing herbs at our homes ensures that they are devoid of any fertilizers and chemical exposure. After all, going organic is the trend! Since we are ready to pay extra for organic foods, why not grow some herbs at our own place? One should not mind making a bit of an effort to ensure quality food on the plate—it is reasonably simple and easy.

7. HING (ASAFOETIDA)

Asafoetida is a hard sap extracted from the roots of *ferula* plants that are native to Afghanistan and India. The sap is dried and grounded into the spice that we know and consume as hing.

The spice is well known for its pungent smell owing to a high concentration of sulfur compounds in it. The odour of this spice does blend in with the food, which is why it is advised to use only a pinch of it.

Essential features and benefits

- Loaded with anti-microbial compounds, it is known to fight against intestinal worms.
- It alleviates symptoms of bloating, gas and IBS.
- It treats indigestion and constipation.
- It is excellent in relieving symptoms of asthma and other respiratory issues.

- Asafoetida acts as a natural blood thinner, proving to be an efficient medicinal spice that treats hypertension.
- Power-packed with coumarin, it improves blood flow and prevents the formation of blood clots.
- It treats headaches, common cold and flu.
- It can provide relief from menstrual pain.
- Hing also contains bioactive sulfur compounds that can help in eliminating heavy metal toxicities. Human trials are needed to specifically measure this effect to strengthen the claim.

Add a pinch of wholesome goodness in your meals

- Add hing while tempering various pulses and other vegetarian dishes or fling it in the gravy when they are about to be cooked.
- Toss a pinch of hing in the ginger-honey mix for a magical remedy for your respiratory issues, including asthma, dry cough and bronchitis.

Caution: Use it in minute quantity as it can leave a pungent flavour in the food if added in excess.

8. AJWAIN (BISHOPS'S WEED OR CAROM SEEDS)

Carom seeds found their use in daily cooking due to its distinct aroma and digestive benefits. However, it has been gradually losing its significance. So, let's explore its benefits and usage that we have been neglecting.

Essential features and benefits

- Referred to as *dippaka* in Ayurveda, carom seeds are recognized as a herb that stimulates appetite and has potent digestive properties.
- It treats peptic ulcers, abdominal pain and indigestion.
- It treats symptoms of bloating and gas.
- It improves triglyceride levels, prevents heart attacks and atherosclerosis.
- It helps to provide relief from toothache when swished with lukewarm water after being boiled with 1 teaspoon of salt.
- Carom seeds water has been proven to be beneficial in enhancing the production of milk for breastfeeding mothers and promotes internal healing post-delivery. They exhibit anesthetic properties, improve back pain and strengthen muscles.

Try the goodness of oma water

- Consume carom seeds powder with 1 glass of warm water during bedtime for proper cleansing of the colon and preventing constipation.
- Oma water is one drink that treats indigestion and issues of bloating and gas. This is especially beneficial for pregnant ladies. Prepare oma water by boiling 2 teaspoons of roasted ajwain seeds in water. Filter out the seeds from the mixture and drink the water before it returns to room temperature.
- Add carom seeds in tea to help get relief from indigestion and treat symptoms of overeating, like buildup of intestinal gas, bloating, flatulence and gas pain after a heavy meal. You can drink the tea 25–30 minutes after having such type of meal.

- Add this as an ingredient, while tempering spices in ghee, olive oil or other cooking oil for preparing curry for lentil dishes or other vegetables.

Caution: Pregnant women should consult their obstetrician-gynaecologist before consuming carom seeds or oma water, as it has been believed to cause uterine contraction in some cases. Doctors generally have been in favour of pregnant women consuming carom seeds, but only in a limited amount.

HERBS CURING COLIC IN INFANTS

Infants can sometimes cry repeatedly for prolonged periods of time for no apparent reason, a phenomenon described as colic. Though there is no definite answer, indigestion and taking in some amount of air while taking a feed are believed to be primary reasons why a child can develop colic. Whatever the root cause may be, the baby will appear to have some kind of abdominal pain, referred to as colic pain. This causes babies to cry relentlessly, pulling their legs upward towards the stomach reflexively.

As much discomfort a kid suffers, it is equally frustrating for the parents to watch them cry inconsolably. But here's some good news for couples who are about to have a baby or who have recently become parents. Next time, when you see your child crying continuously for no apparent reason and showing signs of abdominal discomfort, do not panic or get frustrated with helplessness. You have magical ingredients in your kitchen in the form of ajwain and hing, which can come to your rescue. Try one of the few methods listed below to see the results.

1. Boil 1–2 teaspoons of ajwain in half a glass of water. Keep it boiling till the volume is reduced to half. Allow

it to rest for a few minutes till it becomes lukewarm and suitable to drink. Give 1–2 teaspoons of this water to your child.

2. Also, you can simply roast ajwain. When the seeds turn lukewarm, put them on the navel of your baby.

3. You may heat hing powder and apply it on your kid's tummy.

4. Another alternative includes tempering carom seeds or hing in the mustard oil and applying the lukewarm oil on the navel.

5. Else, you can take a few pinches of hing and add a little water to it, making a paste out of it. Apply the paste with a finger around your baby's navel area in a circular motion. Try to cover the entire area of the abdomen gradually moving away from the navel.

9. HARI MIRCH (GREEN CHILLI)

Green chili is a hot spice grown all over the world. It not only adds a warmth and a spicy taste to our diet but also imparts a spectrum of health benefits ranging from vision and digestion to cardiovascular and immunity.

Essential features and benefits

- It meets the daily iron requirement in our body.
- Packed with dietary fibre, it promotes digestive health.
- Loaded with Vitamin C and beta carotene, it promotes vision health and boosts immunity.
- It improves cholesterol and triglyceride levels, thereby preventing heart attacks and reducing the likelihood of developing atherosclerosis.

- It regulates blood sugar levels.
- Capsaicin in green chillies exhibits a stimulating effect on the mucus membranes of the nose and sinuses, which proves to be beneficial in fighting against common cold and sinus infections.
- It is possessed with antibacterial properties, facilitates in detoxifying the blood, thereby aiding the treatment of skin infections.
- Green chilli releases endorphins that contribute towards boosting your mood.

Spice it up!

Include some spicy flavour and healthy benefits to your food by:

- Adding finely chopped green chilli in cooked lentil dishes, scrambled eggs and omelettes
- Adding green chilli while making purée for gravy of vegetables. The purée may include onions, tomatoes, garlic and/or coriander leaves.
- Eating raw chillies, but in little amounts, with your meals

Caution: Overeating green chillies can result in mouth ulcers and diarrhoea.

10. SAUNF (FENNEL)

Commonly used as a mouth freshener after a meal, fennel is a sweet-tasting spice that is used as a flavouring agent in many Asian cuisines, especially in desserts. It is widely recognized for its digestive and cooling properties. It imparts many more health benefits that you may know of.

Essential features and benefits

- It freshens breath.
- It improves digestion, reduces abdominal bloating and gas.
- Being antispasmodic, it helps in treating abdominal cramps.
- It carries a blend of powerful plant compounds and antioxidants like anethole, exhibiting anti-cancerous properties.
- It protects the internal organs from toxins released during metabolic processes.
- It increases the nitrite content in saliva, boosting the production of nitric oxide in the linings of the blood vessels, thereby keeping a check on high blood pressure.
- It helps in decreasing LDL (bad) cholesterol inside the body.
- Fennel tea serves as an efficient diuretic,[35] supporting kidneys to function more effectively by removing excess fluids and wastes. It also prevents the risk of catching a urinary tract infection.
- Fennel seeds impart a cooling effect on the body, by calming down the nerves and promoting mental clarity.

Relax your organs and senses

- Consume fennel tea after a heavy dinner to help digest food and flush out excess fluids.
- Have a pinch of raw fennel seeds after meals to get rid of bad breath.
- Add fennel seeds in your refreshment drinks and smoothies to relax your body and mind.

---

[35]A diuretic promotes increased production of urine.

- Incorporate fennel seeds as a supplementary condiment in curries and rice dishes.

11. METHI (FENUGREEK)

Popularly known as methi in India, fenugreek is an ancient herb used since 4000 BC in the Middle East. For cooking purposes, you can use its seeds (methi daana), fresh leaves (methi) and dried leaves (kasuri methi).

It is recommended to roast the seeds before using them in a dish to reduce the bitterness and enhance the aromatic flavour. If you want to use methi as a supplement, for making a spice mix, or pickles, prefer buying dried leaves from the market and crush them using a mortar and pestle just before adding them in your recipes.

Essential features and benefits

- Both seeds and leaves serve as blood purifiers, flushing out the toxins and waste from our bodies.
- The seeds and leaves are packed with dietary fibre, which helps in cleansing the intestines.
- Both seeds and leaves are anti-inflammatory in nature, significant in treating arthritis.
- Fenugreek seeds have been clinically established as one of the most potent and efficient spices in down-regulating blood sugar levels. They have been used as oral hypoglycemic agents in naturopathy to treat and cure diabetes. They work by improving insulin sensitivity and reducing insulin resistance, thus enhancing sugar metabolism.
- Drinking water soaked with fenugreek seeds stimulates

lactation, thereby enhancing milk production in breastfeeding mothers. Furthermore, it also spurs the production of testosterone in men, therefore it is effective in boosting libido. In fact, fenugreek is among the top aphrodisiac herbs and spices.

- Nutritionists have long been advocating the use of fenugreek seeds to promote weight loss, liver function, kidney health and improve overall metabolism.
- Fenugreek leaves are rich in folate, increasing the numbers of healthy red blood cells and preventing anaemia.
- The leaves are also rich in vitamins C and K and calcium, enhancing immunity, promoting bone health and preventing the risk of osteoporosis.

The multiple uses of fenugreek

- Traditionally, the fresh leaves are used during winter in North India in staple dishes like aloo methi, palak methi and carrot methi.
- Roast the fresh green leaves to use them while preparing salads.
- Soak fenugreek seeds in a glass of water overnight to reap the most out of them. Drink the water and consume seeds along with it first thing in the morning after brushing.
- Methi daana is an essential ingredient in home-made garam masala, which is added while making starchy vegetables, thick gravies and raitas for a flavoursome meal.
- Add kasuri methi as a flavouring condiment in the curries of various lentil dishes and vegetables. It goes well with root or starchy vegetables like potatoes, radish and carrots.
- Use dried leaves and seeds of fenugreek in preparation of pickles and spice mixes like sambhar powder.

- Incorporate dried fenugreek leaves to the whole wheat dough to make colourful and flavoursome rotis and paranthas.

Caution: Pregnant women are advised not to consume methi leaves as it is known to induce labour. Furthermore, always try to limit your fenugreek intake as overeating may cause nausea and abdominal discomfort.

12. IMLI (TAMARIND)

Tamarind is a tropical fruit that is not only native to Africa and the Middle East but also grows in the Indian subcontinent. Anthropologists have been disputing over who introduced this sour and tangy superfood in India. Some records suggest it was the Ethiopians, while others indicate that it was the Arabs.[36] Nevertheless, tamarind offers a lot of medicinal properties, which need to be highlighted. So, when you see this unattractive fruit next time, do not regard it as simply another flavouring agent.

Essential features and benefits

- It is a rich source of magnesium and potassium, imparting an array of health benefits from regulating blood pressure to controlling sugar levels.
- It is loaded with antioxidants, helps in reducing LDL (bad)

---

[36]N.C. Shah, 'Tamarindus Indica—Introduction in India and Culinary, Medicinal, and Industrial Uses, *Asian Agri-History* Vol. 18, No. 4, 2014, p: 343–355, https://www.asianagrihistory.org/pdf/articles/nc-shah-18-4.pdf. Accessed on 20 December 2021.

cholesterol and triglycerides and helps boost cardiac health.
- The extract of tamarind seeds has been found to inhibit tumour growth. This extract contains a potent blend of antioxidants and phytochemicals, exhibiting powerful anti-inflammatory attributes. It is helpful in specifically improving kidney and pancreatic health and protecting against cancers in renal cells and the pancreas.
- It alleviates gastrointestinal symptoms, treating constipation and stomach ulcers.
- Sucking on pods of raw tamarind comes in handy in providing relief from pregnancy-related nausea and morning sickness.
- It possesses antimicrobial properties to fight against a diverse range of bacteria and parasites, and helps in killing intestinal worms.

Pucker up for the wholesome goodness of tamarind

- Tamarind pulp is widely used while cooking South Indian dishes as well as Mexican, Middle Eastern and Caribbean cuisine. The seeds and leaves are also edible.
- Incorporate tamarind in a variety of sauces, marinades, chutneys, drinks and desserts. It is one of the essential ingredients used for making Worcestershire sauce.
- Eat or suck raw tamarind pods.
- Use this fruit to add a sour note to savoury dishes.
- Make tamarind juice and consume it as a refreshing drink to beat the scorching heat of summers.

Note: As it is high in calories, try to limit your tamarind intake.

Recipe for imli ki chutney (saunth)

Sweet and sour imli ki chutney is a lip-smacking sauce made using tamarind and other spices. It is part of Indian cuisine and a must for making chaat. But do not underestimate this supplement sauce. It offers all the benefits of its invaluable ingredients with a zesty twist of taste.

Ingredients

- 1 cup of seedless tamarind
- ½ cup of small pieces of jaggery
- 1 teaspoon of grated ginger
- 1 teaspoon of roasted jeera powder
- 1 teaspoon of red chilli powder
- ½ teaspoon of black salt
- 1 teaspoon of hing
- Salt to taste

Method

i.   Soak the tamarind in 3 cups of boiled water for 20 minutes, or directly boil the tamarind in the said amount of water for 10 minutes.

ii. Mash the tamarind pods using hands and strain it through a soup strainer.

iii. Discard the leftover tamarind pulp and keep the water.

iv. Add all the ingredients to the tamarind water. Cook the mixture on medium heat for 10–12 minutes until the jaggery melts entirely. Meanwhile, keep stirring the mix at regular intervals.

v.   Once it is done, switch off the flame and allow it to rest and cool.

vi. Transfer the chutney in a clean glass jar and refrigerate. It can be used for up to three months. Serve it with bhel poori or some other kind of chaat.

Note: The saunth thickens on cooling. So, try to keep the consistency of the chutney a little thin.

Recipe for tamarind seeds in buttermilk

Roasted and peeled-off tamarind seeds were a favoured snacking option amongst the Mangaloreans until a few decades back. The seeds have been traditionally considered to be nutritious, and treat indigestion and constipation. Until a few decades ago, a common and ingenious practice among Mangaloreans was transforming roasted tamarind seeds into amazingly soft and tasty morsels using buttermilk.

Ingredients

- 1 cup of rinsed tamarind seeds
- Buttermilk to soak the seeds
- Salt to taste

Method

i. Roast the tamarind seeds until they become aromatic and turn darker in colour. Switch off the flame and allow them to cool to room temperature.

ii. Gently crush the seeds using a mortar and pestle to crack their outer coating. Peel off the seed coat and discard them. Transfer the peeled seeds to a bowl.

iii. Pour enough buttermilk into the bowl to cover the seeds and add in some salt to taste. Cover the bowl and let the mixture rest for 12–24 hours at room temperature until the seeds have softened.

iv. As the seeds soften, keep the bowl in the fridge for about a couple of hours. Serve and consume it cold for a refreshing taste.

v. You can refrigerate any leftovers of the same in an airtight container for up to two to three weeks.

13. ELAICHI (CARDAMOM)

Cardamom is a cooling spice and known since centuries for its culinary and medicinal properties. This aromatic condiment is native to the evergreen rainforest of the southern Indian state of Kerala and grown in only a few tropical countries.

Essential features and benefits

- It is clinically proven that it helps in lowering blood pressure.
- One of its ancient usages has been the treatment of indigestion and nausea, for which it has been used since thousands of years.
- Studies on mice and human cancer cells[37] have indicated that cardamom, in the form of a powder, helps to prevent

[37]Ila Das, Asha Acharya, Deborah L. Berry, Supti Sen, Elizabeth Williams, Eva Permaul, Archana Sengupta, Sudin Bhattacharya, Tapas Saha, 'Antioxidative Effects of the Spice Cardamom Against Non-Melanoma Skin Cancer by Modulating Nuclear Factor Erythroid-2-Related Factor 2 and NF-κB Signalling Pathways', *British Journal of Nutrition*, 108(6), 2012, p: 984–97.

the growth of tumour cells.[38]

- It contains an abundance of antioxidants, protecting cells from oxidative damage and maintaining cellular integrity.
- It is extremely efficient in inhibiting the activity of inflammatory compounds found inside the body of humans, thereby diminishing the risk of chronic ailments.
- It helps prevent bad breath and cavities.
- Cardamom extract has been shown to reduce elevated liver enzymes, triglyceride and cholesterol levels, protecting liver and preventing risk of non-alcoholic fatty liver disease.

Enjoy the unique flavour and aroma

- Consume a pod of raw cardamom as a mouth freshener after having a meal.
- Add it in rice while cooking or in desserts to have unique flavour and aroma.
- Include the ingredient in your home-made chai masala and consume it with your daily tea.
- Use the whole or split pods while cooking traditional meals, like pulses.
- Fry the seeds before adding other ingredients of a dish, or pound them with other spices as needed.
- Purchase cardamom extract oil from a reputed brand and use it as directed in your flavouring dips, tea and desserts.

---

[38]Samir Qiblawi, Mohd Adnan Kausar, S.M.A. Shahid, Mohd Saeed, Awfa Y. Alazzeh, 'Therapeutic Interventions of Cardamom in Cancer and Other Human Diseases', *Journal of Pharmaceutical Research International*, 32, 2020, p: 74–78.

14. LAUNG (CLOVE)

Cloves are obtained as flower buds that are plucked or harvested in their immature state and then dried for use. Widely regarded as a sweet and aromatic spice, clove is mainly used as a flavouring ingredient imparting earthy and warm scent in the food.

Essential features and benefits

- It is rich in manganese, helps improve cognitive function and in building bone strength.
- It is packed with loads of antioxidants, reducing oxidative stress, thereby preventing the risk of cancer and other chronic diseases encompassing cardiometabolic syndrome. These diseases include obesity, hypertension, hyperlipidemia and diabetes.
- It exhibits anti-bacterial properties, promoting oral and gut health.
- Keeping a piece of clove in between your teeth can serve as a remedy for toothache and gum pain.
- Cloves contain eugenol, a compound that has been shown to reverse the scarring of liver caused during hepatic cirrhosis.[39]
- It helps regulate blood sugar levels.

The harbinger of flavour

Known for its versatility as a culinary spice, clove can be used while making various delicacies.

---

[39]Cirrhosis is a liver disease at an advanced stage wherein healthy liver tissue is scarred and the liver is considered to be permanently damaged.

- While cooking rice and desserts, use clove to bring unique flavour and aroma.
- Use cloves in traditional Indian curries of Punjabi, Rajasthani, Bengali or South Indian cuisine as well as in chicken curry recipes.
- Use it for seasoning pot roasts.
- Using them in preparing sambhar.
- Use as a flavouring ingredient in hot beverages and in your daily tea.

Note: Do not feed too many cloves to children under the age of 13. Limit their clove intake as eugenol can prove to be toxic for kids when consumed in high amounts. However, it is quite safe when taken in low quantities.

15. DALCHINI (CINNAMON)

Cinnamon is a warm spice that exhibits a hot and sweet-smelling taste. Mainly used as an aromatic ingredient, it adds a complimenting flavour to sweet and savoury dishes, tea, cereals and traditional foods. But don't be fooled by its honey flavour for it is actually helpful in controlling diabetes and imparts many other medicinal benefits.

Essential features and benefits

- It has powerful anti-inflammatory properties, can repair tissue damage and cut the risk of cardiovascular disorders by half.
- It lowers the level of LDL (bad) cholesterol while keeping HDL (good) cholesterol level stable.
- Loaded with potent antioxidants, it helps prevent the

growth of tumour cells and reduce the risk of cancer.

- It improves insulin sensitivity, thereby, preventing and even reversing the progression of diabetes.
- It helps in enhancing metabolism, making it more robust, thereby promoting weight loss.

INTERESTING FACTS

In one of the major studies, cinnamon was ranked the best spice in terms of having the most potent antioxidant activity. It even outperformed superfoods like garlic and oregano.[40]

Companies making herbal and Ayurvedic supplements have been using the combination of cinnamon and berberine in their products to manage diabetes, dyslipidemia and obesity. These supplements regulate blood glucose and cholesterol levels and boost overall metabolism.

Sprinkle some on your food

- Relish the goodness of cinnamon with a cupful of cinnamon-ginger tea.
- Include the ingredient in and consume it daily with your home-made masala chai.
- Use cinnamon powder as an additive sprinkled on the top of toast or cold coffee.
- Use whole cinnamon in traditional Indian curries of Punjabi, Rajasthani, Bengali and South Indian cuisine as well as in chicken curry recipes.

---

[40]Bin Shan B., Yizhong Z. Cai, Mei Sun, Harold Corke, 'Antioxidant Capacity of 26 Spice Extracts and Characterization of Their Phenolic Constituents', *Journal of Agricultural and Food Chemistry*, 5;53(20), October 2005, p: 7749-59.

- Cinnamon powder goes well with desserts like coffee cake, fruit cake and rice puddings.

Note: Use cinnamon in moderate amount only. Never consume raw cinnamon powder alone as it can block respiratory pathways temporarily, causing severe whooping cough.

Make a tonic with cinnamon and apple cider vinegar

Apple cider vinegar imparts a plethora of direct benefits to the gut, nurturing the beneficial microbiota. It does so by balancing the pH (acidic content) level of our bodies, signalling the gut to secrete the required acids to properly digest the food and eliminate the wastes.

Therefore, combining apple cider vinegar with cinnamon and ginger is like icing on a cake. This tonic is simple to make, requiring the mixing of just four ingredients.

Ingredients

- 1 teaspoon of raw apple cider vinegar
- 1 teaspoon of raw honey
- ½ teaspoon of ground cinnamon
- ½ teaspoon of ginger juice
- 1 cup of filtered water

Method

i.   Boil ½ cup of water.
ii. Take another ½ cup of water and combine all the ingredients and stir them well.
iii. Add boiling water to the mix. The tonic should be at a

perfect temperature to drink. Savour the elixir!

iv. You may add a pinch of sea salt according to your taste.

Note: Do not boil all water content to avoid killing all the beneficial attributes of the apple cider vinegar and the honey.

16. JAIPHAL (NUTMEG)

Nutmeg comes from a tropical evergreen tree, and is indigenous to Indonesia, India and Sri Lanka. Its seeds are shelled, dried and ground into a powder form, which we typically use in kitchen. Although it's more commonly used for its flavour, nutmeg carries a variety of impressive and potent compounds that help to prevent diseases and promote your overall health.

Essential features and benefits

- Nutmeg comes with a power-punch of plenty of antioxidants, preventing oxidative stress, thereby, significantly reducing the risk of cancer.
- The blend of antioxidants also facilitates the reversal of disorders encompassing cardiometabolic syndrome. These include hypertension, diabetes, dyslipidemia, etc.
- It also contains potent anti-inflammatory compounds, which help in promoting cardiac health and significantly reducing swelling of joints among patients of arthritis.
- Nutmeg can exhibit stimulatory effects in boosting libido and enhancing sexual drive and performance.
- It is also shown to have specific antibacterial properties against microbes, causing dental cavities and gum disease, thereby promoting oral health.

Goes with dessert and chai too

- Add freshly grated nutmeg in various kinds of desserts like kheer, cheesecakes, phirni, etc.
- Add a pinch of sharp flavour to your fresh fruit salad, oatmeal or yogurt.
- Add grated nutmeg in garam masala, chai masala, home-made chutney and in beverages like apple cider and smoothies.
- Roast the whole nutmeg seed and crush it to make its powder. Add the powder while preparing marinades, soups and stews.

Caution: Consume nutmeg in small quantities only as it can cause hallucinations or loss of muscle coordination when taken in large amounts.

17. CHAKR PHOOL (STAR ANISE)

The unusual-looking star-shaped spice is a fruit from a small oriental tree native to China. The fruit is picked before it ripens, dried and then sold as a spice. It imparts a sharp flavour and delightful fragrance to the cooked food.

Essential features and benefits

- Densely supplied antioxidants and other bioactive compounds contribute to antimicrobial properties of star anise. This makes the spice a potential ingredient to prevent and treat numerous viral, bacterial and fungal infections.
- Resolves the issues of indigestion, abdominal cramps and nausea.

- It also helps in treating the symptoms of bloating, gas and constipation.
- Drinking one glass of water infused with the crushed seeds of star anise can improve sex drive.

INTERESTING FACTS

One of the prominent and most successful antiviral medications, Tamiflu, contains shikimic acid. This acid is extracted from the pods of star anise, imparting the spice with some potent antiviral properties.

Buckle-up for the goodness

- Add whole star anise while cooking rice dishes, like pulao and biryani.
- Incorporate pods of the spice while preparing marinades, soups and stews for a warming boost of flavour.
- It is a commonly used ingredient in Chinese red cooking.
- Use powdered star anise while making garam masala, or home-made sauces.
- Steep in water to make tea for treating symptoms of nausea, constipation and other digestive issues.
- Star anise also makes a great addition to sweet dishes and desserts. Sprinkle some powdered anise over baked fruit-mix, pies, bread and muffins.

Note: Remember that a little goes a long way when it comes to using star anise. Avoid using it too much. As a precaution, start with small amounts and gradually add more according to your taste.

8

UNDERESTIMATED VALUABLE VEGETABLES

VEGETABLES ARE YOUR BEST BUDDIES

There's a common saying that friends are the family we choose. Most often, we make friends by bonding over talking, eating meals and hanging out together. Parallel to those, there are a few people at our workplace or neighbourhood with whom we have no real interaction. We just know about their existence, but sometimes these people are the ones who help us out at critical times. Often, we do not appreciate their personality and true potential until they aid us in our time of need or provide us with something we are in dire need of. Eventually, we end up knowing them and include them in the circle of our close friends.

Well, this is also how we behave with our friends found in nature—vegetables. While we run after burgers, pizzas and pastas, we do not care about comprehending the significance of vegetables in our health. We realize their importance when we become overweight or diabetic. Then, we start surfing the internet so that we can learn about how to reduce weight. There we find all physicians, dieticians and health bloggers reiterating the benefits of vegetables that we had been neglecting.

Vegetables offer plenty of dietary fibre with complex carbs

and fewer calories, promoting gut health. Therefore, we must not cause any further delay in embracing them. Just like our best friends, they support us in our fight against unwanted elements in the body, uplift our moods and keep us energized. But frying, tempering or sautéing vegetables in refined oil is like fighting with your friend and ruining a beautiful relationship. Consuming them as part of junk food does no good either. Therefore, look out for interesting ways to cook a healthy relationship with vegetables.

WIDEN YOUR FRIEND CIRCLE WITH DIFFERENT VEGETABLES

One of the primary reasons we end up ordering food from outside is because we are bored of having the same type of meal every day. Remember how we like to discuss certain matters with specific friends only? Meanwhile, there are our other friends and colleagues with whom we discuss only family matters, official work, financial strains, love life and so on. Doing so keeps our bond strengthened with everybody. Similarly, we require different kinds of vegetables bringing different benefits in our lives with their own unique advantages.

1. Cruciferous Vegetables

Topping the charts in terms of offering essential nutrients and imparting health benefits is the family of cruciferous vegetables. The most commonly available vegetables in Indian supermarkets among this family are cabbage, cauliflower, broccoli, radish, turnip, brussel sprouts and mustard leaves.

Cross-cultured 'cruciferous' journey

Most of the vegetables belonging to the family of *cruciferae*, like cabbage, cauliflower, broccoli and turnip, are not native in India. They were brought to the subcontinent by merchants during the time of colonization. But gradually, they became a part of our staple diet. Today, India is the second-largest producer of cabbage worldwide. While we adopted and became fond of eating cabbage, cauliflower and radish, we seem to have neglected others like broccoli and turnip.

Why cruciferous vegetables are most preferred by dieticians

- Carrying a potent blend of antioxidants and essential minerals and vitamins, they significantly reduce the risk of chronic ailments, including cardiometabolic syndrome and cancer. Hence, they serve as the ultimate guardians of our health.
- They are better sources of protein than meat and chicken.
- A couple of cruciferous meals will completely meet your daily requirement of omega-3, omega-6 and vitamins B9, C and K.
- A rich source of iron, it helps in increasing haemoglobin count and improving blood flow.
- The bioactive compound in these vegetables is a phytochemical called sulforaphane, which by many research studies,[41] has been proven to have anti-carcinogenic

---

[41]Chhavi Sharma, Lida Sadrieh L., Anita Priyani, Musthaq Ahmed, Ahmad H. Hassan and Arif Hussain, 'Anti-Carcinogenic Effects of Sulforaphane in Association with its Apoptosis-Inducing and Anti-Inflammatory Properties in Human Cervical Cancer Cells', *Cancer Epidemiol*, 35(3), 2011, p: 272-8.

properties.[42] Sulforaphane has been shown to uplift mood, alleviate symptoms of anxiety and depression.

- An excellent source of omega-3 and omega-6, they help promote cardiac health.
- They reduce insulin resistance, preventing and reversing the progression of Type 2 diabetes.
- They exhibit anti-inflammatory properties, promoting nephritic (related to kidneys) and vascular health.

Relish your superfood with super flavours

- Cruciferous vegetables are the most versatile to use. You can cook, steam, roast, fry or stir-fry them.
- Make cruciferous coleslaw for a densely packed nutritious rush.
- Consume them as a lone dish or combine them with other vegetables like potatoes, peas and beans.
- Cook your staple aloo gobi frying it in olive oil. Garnish the dish by tossing coriander leaves and other herbs over it.
- Roast turnips using olive oil. Sprinkle some pepper and mint leaves over it.
- Shalgam ka bharta (mashed turnip) can be a spicy and flavoursome dish even for those who do not usually like eating turnips.
- Next time, make mooli ke paranthe using whole grain flour and olive, or coconut oil, or ghee.
- Try roasting the brussel sprouts using olive oil and onions for a lip-smacking and perfect side dish for just about any occasion.

---

[42] X Su, X. Jiang, L. Meng, X. Dong, Y. Shen, Y. Xin, 'Anticancer Activity of Sulforaphane: The Epigenetic Mechanisms and the Nrf2 Signalling Pathway', *Oxidative Medicine and Cellular Longevity*, 5438179, 2018.

Broccoli, a vegetable that is class apart

Michael Jordan is arguably the best player ever in the history of the NBA. He played for the Chicago Bulls, and his sheer talent helped them win six championships during 1991–1993 and 1996–1998. If you're wondering what happened during 93–94 and 94–95 seasons, well, Jordan did not play during those times. Out of the two seasons that the Bulls did not win, he was not part of the team for a season and a half.

All the gold feathers in the history of the Chicago Bulls are from the time Jordan played for them. They had never won a championship before Jordan, and they could not win it again once he retired in 1998.[43] In short, any conversation about the Chicago Bulls is incomplete without explicitly mentioning him. If one were to write a book on the history of the NBA, they are going to have to dedicate more than a few chapters on Jordan and how he ruled the basketball court, defeated his opponents and helped everybody in his team expand their game.

Similarly, broccoli is the Michael Jordan of the family of the cruciferae. Though all other vegetables in the family carry essential nutrients, the amounts in which broccoli contains these are unparalleled. A conversation about cruciferous vegetables is incomplete without highlighting broccoli.

The broccoli prowess

- Internationally acclaimed chef, the author of multiple books about food, TED speaker, and an active advocate

---

[43]'Legends profile: Michael Jordan', *NBA History*, 14 September 2021, https://www.nba.com/news/history-nba-legend-michael-jordan. Accessed on 20 December 2021.

of sustainable seafood, Barton Seaver, once quoted, 'You want to save more fish? Eat more broccoli.'[44] Such is the nutritional value of the exceptional green.

- A single meal with decent amounts of broccoli can meet your daily requirement of vitamins B9, C and K. This implies that the vegetable can significantly facilitate and assist in
  ○ Proper cellular growth and formation of DNA, especially beneficial for pregnant women
  ○ Enhancing red blood cells count
  ○ Boosting immunity and improving memory and cognitive health
  ○ Maintaining skin tone and overall youthfulness
  ○ Improving iron absorption
  ○ Making wound healing more robust
  ○ Promoting bone health
- It comprises 90 per cent water, keeping your body well hydrated.
- It contains more amounts of dietary fibre and protein than most other vegetables, promoting digestive health, overall gut health and the building of muscular strength.
- It carries a potent blend of antioxidants along with Vitamin C, reducing the risk of cancer and other chronic ailments.
- It is regarded as the best vegetable for uplifting mood and preventing symptoms of anxiety or depression from worsening.
- The vegetable has a decent amount of copper and manganese that improve bone health, significantly reducing the risk of osteoporosis.
- It offers potassium and magnesium, which regulate blood

[44]John Mariani, 'Blue Ridge's Barton Seaver: Chef of the Year', *Esquire*, 12 October 2009.

pressure effectively.

- Omega-3 fatty acids and other bioactive compounds exhibit anti-inflammatory properties, promoting cardiac and neural health in more than one way.

Former teammates of Michael Jordan describe how MJ would bully them during their practice session. However, they acknowledge the fact that they could not have become the players they turned out to be had it not been for him. Now, they thank MJ for those experiences.

You can draw parallels with this aspect of MJ and consuming broccoli as it is not the most palatable vegetable. You do not have to eat them daily; three to four meals in a week will do. But once you regularly start having broccoli, you will begin feeling its positive effects soon.

'Listen to your broccoli and it will tell you how to eat it'

—Anne Lamott

You can add your own flavour to broccoli by combining it with herbs and spices of your choice and still enjoy all the innate qualities that the vegetable has to offer.

You've got to own your broccoli

- Steam broccoli, along with cabbage, to reap the maximum benefits out of them. Adding cabbage will impart a pleasant flavour and a crunchy texture.
- Give your boiled broccoli a dressing of olive oil, combining it with fried onions and finely chopped hard cheese. Sprinkle some salt and pepper for added flavour.
- Temper garlic over low flame using olive oil until it is fragrant. Drizzle some lemon juice and sprinkle salt and

pepper according to your taste. Toss this garlic mix over a bowlful of steamed broccoli for a zesty 'detox' supplement.

- Roast broccoli with cauliflower, carrots or smashed garlic for an exquisite side dish.
- Try experimenting with broccoli by making flavoursome creamy soups along with celery, onions and cheese.
- Give an enticing twist of taste to the humble broccoli with Indian tadka.
  - ○ Sauté chopped garlic and sliced onions in olive oil. Add boiled broccoli to it and stir-fry the mix for a wholesome dish. Sprinkle salt, coriander powder, red chilli powder and garam masala according to your taste for added flavours.
  - ○ Use olive oil and temper whole cumin seeds (jeera), mustard seeds, crushed garlic, green chilli and onions. Toss a few curry leaves and add turmeric, salt, garam masala and coriander powder. In the end, add finely chopped tomatoes and mix it well to finish making a flavoursome masala. Cover the pan for two minutes to let the flavours and aroma blend well. Add boiled broccoli to it and mix it well. Pour half a glass of water for gravy. Stir the mix well for two to three minutes till it thickens. Serve and relish the tempting dish after garnishing it with coriander leaves.

2. Drumsticks

Drumsticks, also known as moringa, have been recognized as one of the modern-day superfoods. With a plethora of health benefits ranging from developing bone strength to boosting immunity, it is a vegetable we must focus on and include in our daily meals.

Essential features and benefits

- It exhibits powerful anti-inflammatory properties and contains generous amounts of Vitamin C that not only treats symptoms of respiratory disorders but also helps to boost immunity.
- It is a rich source of calcium and iron that helps in building bone strength.
- It is loaded with potent antioxidants, preventing the growth of tumour cells and reducing the risk of cancer.
- It revamps libido and sexual drive, particularly in men.
- It helps improve insulin sensitivity, thereby regulating blood sugar levels.
- Packed with dietary fibre, it promotes digestive health.
- It is one of the very few vegetables that help in purifying blood.

Enjoy the stick

- Add plenty of drumsticks in your traditional South Indian curries, especially sambhar.
- Do not hesitate to include them in meat or chicken curries as well.
- Make soups using them.
- Try experimenting by adding them in yellow-coloured dals.
- Use them as an essential ingredient in soups, salads and sauces for a crispy and crunchy touch.

Ingredients for drumstick soup

- 4–5 drumsticks
- 2 cups of water
- 1 teaspoon of cumin seeds, salt and black pepper

Method

i. Chop 4–5 immature drumsticks (the ones in which no seeds have formed) and boil them in 2 cups of water.

ii. Add a teaspoon each of cumin seeds, salt and black pepper. Strain the vegetable and drink the soup. This recipe helps men boost their libido.

3. Lotus root

Lotus root, as the name suggests, is derived from the lotus plant. It is extremely versatile as a vegetable in the sense that it can be steamed, baked, grilled, braised or fried. Lotus root imparts a crunchy texture and slightly sweet taste, making it a relishing ingredient. With a past where it was used in traditional medicine for centuries, let's look at its primary benefits and how we can incorporate it into our modern-day cooking.

Essential features and benefits

- Loaded with Vitamin B complex, it helps in reducing stress and headaches.
- Improving insulin sensitivity, it helps regulate blood sugar
- levels.
- Packed with dietary fibre, it enhances digestive capabilities.
- It is rich in potassium, which regulates blood pressure, thereby helping in treating hypertension.
- Potassium in lotus root also serves to increase urine production and helps to prevent excess water retention. As the fluid drains out of the body, it stimulates weight loss, which is especially beneficial for people suffering from morbid obesity.

- The presence of vitamins B and C helps in boosting immunity and improving health of our skin and hair.

Add a crunchy bite to your diet

- Boil lotus roots for 10 minutes and then eat them to kick-start your day.
- Fry some lotus roots in olive oil or coconut oil and enjoy as an evening snack.
- Stir-fry lotus roots with sesame seeds and green onion to prepare a delicious dish. The recipe can be easily found on the internet.
- Add raw lotus roots in mixed vegetable soups.
- Prepare crispy baked lotus root chips.

Note: Do not use refined oil while frying or baking lotus roots as it kills the purpose of healthy snacking. Use sesame or olive oil.

4. Green Banana

Simply put, the green banana is an unripe form of banana which is harvested before its starch gets converted into simple sugars like glucose. Devoid of sugars, green banana tastes slightly bitter, has a firm texture and serves as an excellent feed for the good bacteria living in the gut.

Essential features and benefits

- It carries the maximum amount of resistant starch than rice or any other fruit, providing a sense of fullness after consumption. Hence, it aids in losing weight.
- With an abundance of complex starch and almost no sugar,

the consumption of raw banana keeps blood glucose levels in check. This is why dieticians highly recommend this food to their diabetic patients.

- It serves as an excellent source of prebiotics, promoting gut health and treating various kinds of digestive issues.
- It is loaded with potassium, which regulates blood pressure, thereby helping in treating hypertension, improving kidney function and supporting weight loss.

Don't you be resistant towards this starchy delight

- Boil green bananas for 15 minutes and consume them by sprinkling a pinch of pepper and salt over them.
- Include green banana in traditional sautéed dishes like vazhakkai poriyal (raw banana plantain curry).
- Savour some mouth-watering recipes like coconut kachori with raw banana, kele ki sabzi, raw banana kebab, etc.

Note: Resistant starch is a complex carbohydrate that is biochemically folded compactly and is not entirely absorbed by our bodies. In simple terms, it is a kind of complex carbohydrate, which we discussed earlier in the book. This starch is turned into short-chain fatty acids (SCFAs) by intestinal bacteria.

These SCFAs exhibit tremendous benefits for our overall health, which include, but are not limited to, the following:

- Nourishing the GI tract (gut) lining, improving absorption of nutrients and reversing the effects of inflammation
- Stimulating better immune response, boosting immunity
- Treating issues related to indigestion

5. Raw Jackfruit (kathal)

Hailed as one of the superfoods, jackfruit is a unique tropical fruit native to South India. Raw jackfruit is harvested four to five days before it ripens completely and turns sweet. Many South Indians love it as a fruit and its seed as a protein-rich nut. In the north, tender jackfruit or kathal is eaten as a gourmet vegetable. Raw jackfruit, also referred to as *chakka*, serves an alternate to rice and roti, which people enjoy with curry recipes.

Essential features and benefits

- The high water and dietary fibre content in it provide quick satiation, which helps in managing appetite and thus supports weight loss.
- It is an excellent source of many anti-inflammatory compounds that help in alleviating cholesterol levels and reducing the risk of other chronic diseases.
- Having a low glycemic load, consumption of raw jackfruit does not cause a surge in blood sugar levels, which is especially beneficial for diabetic patients.
- Moreover, a decent amount of magnesium improves insulin sensitivity, preventing diabetes in those who consume raw jackfruit regularly.
- It is loaded with potent antioxidants and helps in preventing the risk of colon cancer.
- It promotes youthfulness and enhances longevity.
- It serves as a powerhouse of vitamins A and C, thereby boosting immunity.
- It contains potassium and magnesium that help in regulating blood pressure effectively.
- Blend of copper and manganese improves bone health, significantly reducing the risk of osteoporosis.

Switch to jackfruit today

- Enjoy the soft fleshy texture of jackfruit as a substitute for eating meat.
- Cherish the benefits of raw jackfruit with fish curry, lentil dishes or vegetable curries, serving as an alternate to roti or rice.
- Prepare a traditional north Indian kathal ki sabzi.
- Include finely cut jackfruit in soups and curries.
- Raw jackfruit goes best with savoury recipes.

6. Sweet Potato (shakarkand)

Sweet potatoes are a starchy root vegetable, slightly sweet and a distant relative of potatoes. They are an excellent source of dietary fibre, multiple vitamins and antioxidants. Exceptionally versatile for cooking, they are one of the easiest additions to our diet, similar to potatoes. They can be grilled, baked, roasted, steamed, fried, stir-fried and what not! With all the resistant starch they have to offer, sweet potatoes present a healthier substitute to potatoes.

Essential features and benefits

- A couple of meals with sweet potato can meet your daily requirement of vitamins A and C, improving vision and boosting immunity significantly, respectively.
- It contains decent amounts of vitamins B5 and B6, facilitating the formation of blood cells and promoting neuronal health, respectively.
- It is densely packed with dietary fibre and complex carbohydrates in the form of resistant starch, enhancing digestive and overall gut health.

- It comes loaded with potent antioxidants, maintaining skin health, brain health and youthfulness.
- It is blended with a mix of sodium and potassium, which keeps your blood pressure levels in check.
- White-skinned sweet potatoes have been shown to improve insulin sensitivity, preventing the risk of diabetes, though more studies on humans are required to confirm these findings.

Gear up for a starchy delight!

- Use chunks of grilled sweet potato in salads, snacks and soups.
- Pair up sweet potato with ginger and apples for a surprising dessert.
- Prepare healthy baked sweet potato chips or fry them after cutting them into matchsticks or wedges.
- Substitute boiled and mashed sweet potato with your regular potato in your sandwiches.
- Make sweet potato hash by peeling, dicing and cooking it with onions in a pan.

Note: Do not use refined oil while frying or baking sweet potatoes as it kills the purpose of healthy snacking. Use olive oil or edible coconut oil.

7. Celery

Celery originates from the family of aromatic flowering plant with its long fibrous stalk tapering into leaves. Both stalks and leaves of celery are edible and used in cooking. It is a low-calorie vegetable with exceptionally high water content, which we can eat raw, cooked, steamed or baked.

Essential features and benefits

- It is loaded with multiple kinds of powerful antioxidants that prevent the growth of tumour cells and help reduce the risk of cancer.
- A dynamic blend of antioxidants with more than 20 anti-inflammatory compounds, it helps in reducing inflammation in organ linings and the entire gut.
- The mix of potent bioactive chemicals facilitates in reversing the progression of arthritis, osteoporosis and stomach ulcers.
- Recognized as a low-calorie food, celery helps in weight management.
- It is one of the best vegetables in terms of enhancing digestive health.
- It serves as a rich source of vitamins and minerals, promoting bone health, improving vision and boosting immunity.

Celery inclusion in your diet

- Use celery in a vegetable salad with radish and beetroot.
- Spread some cheese into the hollow sides of a couple of trimmed celery stalks and then sprinkle it with ¼ cup of assorted dried fruits.
- Prepare smooth, flavoursome and colourful celery soup.
- Search the internet on how to make braised celery as a simple side dish.
- Opt to consume steamed celery as much as possible as that form retains its flavor and nutrients.

Note: Most of the calcium, potassium and Vitamin C are in the leaves. So, do not discard the leaves and eat them within a couple of days after buying from the market as they can't be stored for long.

8. Beetroot (chukandar)

Beetroot is one of the healthiest root vegetables you can ask for imparting vibrant colours (purple-red, pink or yellow) to your meal. Beetroot tastes delicious when eaten raw but is often cooked and pickled as well.

Essential features and benefits

- Beetroot serves as a significant source of dietary fibre with carbohydrates, Vitamin B9, potassium and Vitamin C. It helps in improving digestive health, repairing tissue damage, regulating blood pressure and boosting immunity.
- It offers a decent dose of manganese, promoting bone health and significantly reducing the risk of osteoporosis.
- It is a rich source of iron which helps in increasing the haemoglobin levels.
- It purifies blood and detoxifies the gut effectively.
- It contains pigments called betalains that exhibit several anti-inflammatory properties, potentially reducing kidney and liver inflammation.
- Loaded with potent antioxidants, it helps prevent the growth of tumour cells and reduce the risk of cancer.
- It is known that drinking a couple of glasses of beetroot juice two to three hours before a sports activity enhances athletic performance dramatically with reduced fatigue.
- More than a few studies have shown that regular consumption of beetroot can improve blood flow to the

brain, enhancing working memory and overall cognitive function.[45] [46]

Consume as salad or juice

- Have a crunchy bite with beetroot kebab.
- Add raw beetroot as a salad with at least one of your daily meals.
- Prepare beetroot vegetable to receive a healthy dose of nutrients.
- Relish the smoky flavour of roasted beetroot with a dressing of olive oil. Sprinkle some sea salt and thyme over it. Consume it as a meal on its own or with steamed celery for a low-calorie super breakfast.
- Refresh yourself with soothing and powerful beetroot juice made using lemon, ginger, carrots and celery.
- Include it as an ingredient in your pickles or home-made fermented recipes.

[45]T.D. Presley, A.R. Morgan, E. Bechtold, W. Clodfelter, et al., 'Acute Effect of a High Nitrate Diet on Brain Perfusion in Older Adults', *Nitric Oxide: Biology and Chemistry*, 24(1), 2011, p: 34–42.

[46]Tom Clifford, Glyn Howatson, Daniel J. West and Emma J. Stevenson, 'The Potential Benefits of Red Beetroot Supplementation in Health and Disease', *Nutrients*, 7(4), 2015, p: 2801–2822.

9

FORGOTTEN MILLETS

Widely regarded as one of the most ancient crops, millets are a group of small-grained cereal food crops. They are simply referred to as grains. Highly nutritious, they are used for human consumption and serve as fodder for cattle. Millets are indigenous to many parts of the world, including the Indian subcontinent.

These crops have been favoured due to their adaptability to grow in hot, dry and arid conditions. Millets require low input in terms of water and fertilizers but exhibit high productivity in a short growing season.

The primary grains grown in the largest quantities are referred to as 'major millets'. These include sorghum (jowar) and pearl millet (bajra).

Other grains comprise the class of minor millets, which include:

- Finger millet (ragi/mandua)
- Foxtail millet (kangni/Italian millet)
- Little millet (kutki)
- Barnyard millet (sawan/jhangora)
- Proso millet (cheena/common millet)
- Browntop millet (korale)

GROWN AT LARGE, CONSUMED SCANTILY

Once consumed as a staple food by all in entire Karnataka, Andhra Pradesh and Tamil Nadu, grains like jowar and ragi have almost disappeared from the people's diet in that region. Now, their regular consumption only remains limited to certain rural areas of Karnataka. The same happened with bajra in Rajasthan, Punjab and Haryana. Combining all millets, they constitute only 7 per cent of national food grain basket. This gradual but significant downfall in the consumption of millets is not due to their price or availability. These grains are still harvested with a high yield. In fact, sorghum (jowar) is the third most important crop grown in India in terms of area and production.[47] However, much of the millets produced are used as poultry feed.

SO, WHAT HAPPENED?

As the food industry found out how convenient and cheap it was to process and carry out refinement as far as wheat, rice, sugarcane, corn and soybean were concerned, they significantly increased the production of these crops to use them in the manufacturing of either packed foods or refined oil. They promoted the benefits of only these grains because these were all they could use in their multi-grain or ready-to-prepare food products.

With the Green Revolution, development of irrigation

---

[47] *The Story of Millets*, Karnataka State Department of Agriculture, Bengaluru, India and Indian Institute of Millets Research, Hyderabad, India, 2018, https://www.millets.res.in/pub/2018/The_Story_of_Millets.pdf. Accessed on 20 December 2021.

facilities, growing demand of the fast food industry and public distribution system policies of the government, more farmers started considering the plantation of more wheat, rice, corn and soybean. As a result, these grains reached every household.

On the other hand, lack of knowledge about the health benefits of millets made it lose its opportunity to attract consumers. Moreover, nowadays, the younger generation does not have enough time or knowledge to prepare rotis and other foods from coarse grains of millets. With all of these factors combined, millets continue to drift away towards obscurity.

THE FUTURE, HOWEVER, LOOKS PROMISING

There is a silver lining that has appeared recently in the form of food companies trying to incorporate millets in their multi-grain products. Scientists have been able to highlight and prove the benefits that millets impart. Nutritionists and dieticians concur with those findings and have begun recommending millets as a gluten-free and healthier alternative to refined grains. Many South Indian vegetarian restaurants have started to offer millet versions of upmas, dosas and idlis.

However, till the time the food industry finds a palatable food product at a reasonable rate, it's better to consume the whole grain form of millets and include them in our daily meals. Millets have been a part of the Indian staple diet for centuries, much before rice and wheat. Therefore, we must value the significance of these grains for the nutrition and health benefits they offer.

EXPLORING GOLD NUGGETS OF OUR FOOD ECOSYSTEM

1. **Sorghum** (jowar): Sorghum is world's fifth major cereal food crop in terms of area and production after rice, wheat, maize and barley.[48] One of the staple foods in Karnataka and Andhra Pradesh, it is highly valuable as a healthy grain not only for humans but also as fodder for animals.

JOWAR: THE INDISPENSABLE CROP

Famous plant explorer and archaeobotanist Jack Harlan, hailed jowar as 'one of the really indispensable crops', which is needed for the survival of mankind.[49]

Reasserting the statement

People living in the regions of Ladakh and the upper Himalayas stock jowar in summers. When all the supplies are cut due to blockage of roads with snow in winters, they keep making rotis of jowar and consume them with beef.

2. **Pearl millet** (bajra): Of all the cereal crops, pearl millet has the maximum tolerance for droughts and hot and arid conditions. The grain is warm in nature and is considered as an alternative to wheat, rice and corn, especially in winters. For centuries, it has been a staple food in western Punjab, Haryana and Rajasthan areas.

3. **Finger millet** (ragi): Ragi is a significant primary food, especially for the rural populations of southern India.

---

[48]Ibid.

[49]J.R. Harlan De Wet J.M.J., 'The Origin and Domestication of Sorghum Bicolor', *Economic Botany*, 25, 1971, p: 128–35.

Having the highest productivity per hectare among the millets in India, this variant is one of the richest sources of essential amino acids. The grain has been widely regarded for its use as weaning foods for kids and is served in the form of ragi porridge.

4. **Foxtail millet** (kangni): Kangni is one of the most ancient crops harvested in India, which also finds its mention in some of the oldest Yajurveda scripts as *priyangava*. Significantly less coarse in texture, this grain is the easiest to cook among millets.

Essential features and benefits of millets

- Millets are the richest source of resistant starch. When consumed as whole grain or whole flour, they do not let blood sugars spike after having a meal, thereby preventing and reducing the risk of diabetes.
- Millets are the perfect grains for not only preventing diabetes but also reversing the progression of it. People have come off their anti-diabetic medications in a few weeks after substituting millets for wheat or rice (of course, along with taking other preventive measures).
- The resistant starch and dietary fibre promote overall gut health, improve digestive health and effectively detoxify the colon, etc.
- Millets serve as a rich source of proteins (20 per cent of the daily value), and a variety of micronutrients like manganese, vitamins B1, B3, B6, B9, zinc, etc.
- They also offer plenty of iron, which helps to increase haemoglobin levels.
- Loaded with potent antioxidants, it helps prevent the growth of tumour cells and reduces the risk of cancer.

- It provides quick satiation and supports weight loss.
- It serves as a rich source of essential amino acids for proper growth of cells and tissues.

Go gluten-free with millets

Gluten is a common name referring to a group of proteins that are found to be occurring with starch in many cereal grains, mainly wheat, barley, rye and oats. Inherently, gluten is not considered harmful in general. But this protein evokes adverse autoimmune and inflammatory responses in those who have gluten-sensitivity or coeliac disease. The worst part is that these effects are often not visible. And a lot of people never get to realize that they are reeling under a serious illness.

Coeliac disease, in particular, affects 2 per cent of the population worldwide, causing damage to the small intestine. It has also been strongly linked to causing Type 1 diabetes as a long-term implication.

Millets, being gluten-free, serve as an excellent food for those having coeliac disease, gluten-sensitivity or diabetes.

Historically, people living in South India like the Dravidians have had a lean body and were considered superior warriors. The subsequent generation has also been extremely athletic. Since they did not grow wheat, millets were the staple grains among them, until recently. In the last decade of the twentieth century, wheat came knocking at their doors and substituted millets as their primary food in its refined form.

However, from an evolutionary point of view, these people were not well-equipped to metabolize the higher amounts of simple carbs along with gluten in it. As a result, there was a spike in their blood sugar, and some of it turned into fat.

And South India saw a catastrophic rise in the prevalence of obesity and diabetes.

Moreover, dieticians and bariatric surgeons have seen the after-effects of making their obese patients follow the gluten-free diet. And the results have been amazing! An obese patient can reduce significant body weight within three weeks of following a gluten-free diet. A lot of diabetic patients have been able to stabilize their blood sugars for prolonged periods and gradually come off their medications.

Some unique characteristics of various millets

Each type of millet imparts some unique health benefits, making it stand out from other millets. Let's explore these distinctive qualities in brief.

Sorghum

- It is loaded with a higher fraction of antioxidants than any other cereals or fruits.
- It binds to toxins effectively, which helps in detoxifying the GI tract.
- It is a good source of potassium and devoid of sodium, serves as a potential remedy for treating high blood pressure.

Pearl millet

- It is somewhat bitter in taste and has a coarse texture.
- It is a rich source of healthy phospholipids, plays a vital role in brain function, can treat symptoms of behavioral disorders and reduce stress.
- It helps in regeneration of cell membranes, thereby protecting the linings of the liver, lungs, kidneys and GI tract.

Finger millet

- It contains natural calcium in abundance, which helps in strengthening bones of growing children and aging people, thereby reducing the risk of osteoporosis and fracture
- One of the excellent sources of essential amino acids, it is need for the healthy growth of the body; plays a vital role in many metabolic pathways
- It is widely used as a weaning food, and is believed to support brain development in growing kids.

Foxtail millet

- It helps in boosting brain and cognitive functions, which makes it one of the most essential foods to be given to children from the age of two to five.
- It serves as a rich source of calcium, phosphorus and Vitamin B1, promoting bone health and enhancing immunity.
- It regulates LDL (bad) cholesterol levels and improves good cholesterol levels.

Start including millets in your diet

1. **Ragi porridge:** Wean your babies off breast milk and introduce them to a nutritious and delightful ragi porridge, which includes grain flour, jaggery powder and hot water. As your kid grows older than one, you can add almond or coconut milk, nuts and dates in it. It is also consumed as a standard breakfast by all age groups in many parts of Karnataka and Andhra.
2. **Jowar ke ladoo:** Made by using jowar flour, jaggery powder and a combination of nuts, this delicacy serves as a healthy

snacking option. The laddoos are as tasty as any jowar recipe can get.

3. **Bajre ka halwa:** A winter special, bajre ka halwa is a simple Punjabi delicacy made using whole bajra flour roasted in ghee and then pouring jaggery syrup with added cardamom to it. You can garnish the halwa with finely chopped almonds or cashews.

4. **Barfi from kuttu ka atta:** Kuttu (buckwheat) is a fruit seed, which is why its flour is traditionally used and consumed by people during the fasting days of Navratri. However, the flour can be mixed with that of millets and used in making barfi as a dessert. Kuttu is gluten-free and carries a blend of essential fatty acids that are good for cardiac health. It helps in keeping blood pressure in check and maintaining good cholesterol level.

5. **Making sattu combining millets:** Sattu has its origin in rural areas of Bihar. Traditionally, it is made by roasting Bengal grams (channa dal). However, you can now make multi-grain sattu by roasting different millets like jowar and ragi, along with Bengal gram. Add ghee to the roasted mix and consume it with yogurt or pickle for a wholesome experience. You can also grind the roasted mix to turn it into flour and make parathas from it.

Other alternatives to make the most out of millets are as follows:

Jowar

- Make a tasty roti of jowar using a whole grain flour, substituting it for the one you make from refined flour of wheat.

- Indulge in healthy snacking with popped sorghum in place of popcorns.
- Soothe your taste buds by making upma or khichdi from jowar.
- Do not underestimate the taste of jowar dosa or idlis. It will surprise you. Try it!
- Add sorghum as an ingredient in making mixed vegetable dishes.

Bajra

- Try to include bajre ki roti in at least one of your meals every other day. Make sure that you do not knead the flour of pearl millet into batter all at once beforehand. Prepare the dough for one roti at a time and immediately make a roti using it. If you keep the mix for a long time, you will start seeing cracks in it and it might even turn bitter.
- Relive your tradition with bajre ki khichdi.
- Relish the deliciousness of desserts made from bajra like laddoo and kheer.
- For healthy snacking, roast pearl millets and consume them with some sautéed onions and chili, sprinkling some lemon juice, salt and pepper over it. You can also add almonds or peanuts.
- Have pearl millets as sprouts for a healthy breakfast.

Ragi

- Experiment with ragi roti by adding different herbs and spices to it for a wholesome meal. The recipe of the same can be taken from internet.
- You can also make ragi dosa or idlis.
- Soothe your senses in summers with a refreshing drink of salted ragi ganji made using whole ragi flour, salt, water

and buttermilk.

- Follow the Kannada tradition and relish the wholesome goodness of the simplest of delicacy, ragi mudde. Consume them with sambar or any traditional dal.
- Rotis made from jowar, bajra and ragi taste best when served with vegetable curries or stewed dishes of legumes or lentils.

Kangni

- Indulge in the appeasing flavour of kangni by making upma and khichdi using it.
- Enjoy delicious desserts like kheer or carrot pudding made from kangni.
- Include it as one of the main ingredients in making cucumber salad.
- Use it while making scrambled eggs.

REINSTITUTING AN INDIGENOUS DELICACY USING AMARANTH GRAIN

Amaranth is one of the oldest grown crops that recently came into the limelight as one of the superfoods. Botanically, they are pseudo-cereals with tiny grains, exhibiting a soft and crunchy texture. In comparison to millets, they are simpler to prepare and lighter to digest. Additionally, they can be readily eaten in summers as they are cool from the inside.

MY FAVOURITE: CHAULAI KE LADOO

I have fond memories from childhood when my mom would make chaulai ke ladoo during festival days of Ganesh Chaturthi, Rakhi and Diwali. They looked mouth-watering and were luscious.

Till date, I make them at home on special occasions or sometimes as sweet snacks, reliving old memories. These ladoos are delicious and super easy to make. All you need to do is pop the amaranth seeds and add them to melted/heated jaggery keeping in mind the right consistency. Drench your palms with water and roll the batter into ladoos while it is still warm.

Other uses of amaranth

- The best way to consume amaranth is to roast them and add them to yogurt, along with a few slices of fruits, nuts and cinnamon powder for a healthy cereal in breakfast.
- You can also blend them into your smoothies, soups and stews.
- Being one of the most ancient grains, amaranth is an integral ingredient in the Paleo diet.[50] While following this diet, you can substitute wheat roti with the one made using amaranth.

Benefits

Like millets, amaranth is also absolutely gluten-free! Being high in protein and fibre, its positive effects on weight loss and treating obesity have been clinically proven. Amaranth also contains potent antioxidants, exhibiting anti-inflammatory

---

[50]You can eat meat, fish, eggs, vegetables, fruits, nuts, seeds, herbs, spices and whole grains in natural form. You have to avoid processed foods, sugar, soft drinks, refined grains, most dairy products, artificial sweeteners, vegetable oils and trans-fats.

FORGOTTEN MILLETS • 181

properties, which can control and prevent autoimmune disorders, cancer, diabetes, etc. Highly nutritious, a cup of these cooked grains can meet your entire daily requirement of manganese and significantly fulfill your needs of magnesium, phosphorus, iron, selenium and copper.

MAKE YOUR OWN VEGETABLE BROTH

As you've learned about the unique qualities of various vegetables, herbs and spices, it's time to impart all of their attributes in a single recipe by making a prebiotics-filled, flavoursome and zesty mix-veggie broth.

Ingredients

- 2 onions
- 2 leeks
- A small piece of ginger
- 12–15 garlic cloves
- 1–12 drumsticks
- 3–4 sweet potatoes
- 3–4 beetroots
- Some lotus stems
- Small piece of cabbage
- 2 turnips
- 2 carrots
- Small bunch of celery
- Small bunch of coriander leaves
- 10 cups of water
- 2 teaspoons of olive oil
- Salt as needed
- Pepper as needed

Method

i.   Wash the veggies, including onions and leeks, and chop them finely.

ii. Peel the skin of garlic and ginger. Crush them using mortar and pestle.

iii. Take a heavy and wide bottomed stock pot or vessel, add 2 teaspoons of olive oil in it and throw in the crushed garlic and ginger with finely chopped onions and leeks.

iv. Sauté the mix over medium flame for a couple of minutes.

v.   Add all the veggies and mix well.

vi. Pour a few cups of water and let the mix simmer for an hour or so.

vii. Now add the coriander leaves and salt.

viii. Let the mix boil. As soon as it starts boiling, cover the vessel and let the broth simmer on low flame for another 45 minutes to an hour.

ix. Then switch off the flame and allow it to cool.

x.   You can consume the mix immediately (along with veggies) or filter out the vegetables to only drink the broth. You can keep the broth refrigerated for three to four days in a clean box to consume it later.

10

POWERFUL FRUITS

We have all gone to someone's house carrying a basket of fruits, especially when we are visiting to see someone sick, haven't we? Yes, it might be a tradition but it's also because we consider them a healthy, wholesome option that can be consumed easily. Fruits are loaded with micronutrients that replenish many deficiencies and maintain overall well-being. However, we do not go beyond considering apples, mangoes, grapes, bananas and a few others. Though these fruits offer micronutrients in some amounts, they also contain a significant amount of sugar. Consider fruits as vegetables with plenty of sugar in it.

This is why we must talk about healthier options in the fruit category as well. In this chapter, we'll talk about the health benefits of fruits that have a low glycemic load (discussed in previous chapters) and can be eaten in moderate amounts. We will discuss papayas, melons, peaches, pomegranates, etc., while showing how one can relish their benefits in the form of smoothies, salads, puddings, desserts and much more.

The chapter will also help you move on from exotic berries, like strawberries, that are expensive to buy and not commonly available. We will talk about indigenous berries that are equally healthy and nutritious, including rasbhari, amla, jamun, etc. The chapter also highlights some other forgotten indigenous fruits like karonda, phalsa, kokum and bael fruit, which have lost popularity over the years but are still widely consumed in certain parts of India. These fruits can be used to make refreshing beverages, as you will learn ahead.

1. PAPAYA

Papaya is botanically a type of large berry with a unique smell. It is soft when completely ripened.

Essential features and benefits

- It has powerful anti-inflammatory properties, which helps in reducing the risk of cardiometabolic diseases.
- It is high in dietary fibre and contains an enzyme called papain, significantly improving digestion.
- It is loaded with potent antioxidants, preventing the growth of tumour cells and reducing the risk of cancer.
- It makes your skin look more toned and promotes overall skin health.
- Fermented papaya serves as an excellent source of prebiotics, which improves gut health, reverses inflammation and helps fight infections.

Add papaya to your meals

- Fill your belly with the goodness of papaya, yogurt, oats and chopped nuts for a satisfying breakfast. You can cut papaya into two-halves, remove the seeds, add yogurt into the cupped space of the fruit, and then add oats, berries and chopped nuts as fillings.

- Consume papaya half an hour before your meal as an appetizer.
- Relish the complimenting taste of papaya in a salsa, including chopped tomatoes, onions and cilantro. Add lime juice and mix the ingredients well to enjoy the delicacy.
- Soothe your senses with a smoothie made from diced papaya and coconut milk and blend them well in a blender with ice.
- Add raw papaya in a fruit salad with a pinch of pepper or salt.
- Make a delicious dessert by combining chopped fruits with 2 tablespoons of chia seeds, 1 cup of almond milk and ¼ teaspoon of vanilla. Mix well and refrigerate before eating.
- Consume fermented papaya as an excellent source of prebiotics.

DID YOU KNOW?

Papain is a proteolytic enzyme, which breaks down long protein chains within foods, thereby aiding in digestion. It makes papaya an excellent remedy to treat constipation and symptoms of IBS.

2. COCONUT AND COCONUT WATER

Loosely speaking, coconut can be either referred to as a fruit, nut or a seed. However, botanists like to recognize it as a one-seeded drupe. Extremely fibrous in nature, every element of a coconut has its significance, of which we shall explore about two: the white flesh referred to as kernel and the water it contains.

Essential features and benefits

- The white flesh of coconut has an abundance of dietary fibre promoting digestive health.
- With high levels of manganese, the coconut kernel is extremely beneficial for bone health and proper metabolism of macronutrients like protein and carbohydrates.
- It contains a blend of potent antioxidants, promoting cardiac health and preventing cellular damage from oxidative stress or chemotherapy.
- It diminishes LDL (bad) cholesterol while maintaining good cholesterol level.
- Coconut water is rich in potassium and devoid of sodium, which can help in reducing blood pressure.

Antiviral potency of coconut water

- It has been found that viruses do not survive in an alkaline environment (with a pH greater than seven).
- Drinking coconut water helps driving the pH of the stomach and gut towards the alkaline state, preventing viral infection and killing the virus if you have contracted one.
- Our stomach secretes various acidic fluids that are critical to digesting food, which is why it is advised not to drink coconut water right after a meal. Drink it on an empty stomach.

Add some magic of coconut

- Include raw kernel of coconut in your fruit salad in moderate amounts.

- Sprinkle some grated coconut in your oatmeal with yogurt.
- Refresh, re-energize and rehydrate yourself by drinking pure coconut water. It is preferred that you drink the water straight from a coconut. Otherwise, make sure you buy 100 per cent pure coconut water with no added sugar.
- Add grated coconut in desserts like kheer and different types of halwa.
- Garnish your smoothies and other refreshment drinks with grated coconut.
- Relish the taste of coconut by making a variety of traditional South Indian dishes like avial or kurma.
- You can also buy coconut milk from the market and prepare coconut curry using various herbs and spices.
- Alternatively, you can make a creamy mixed vegetable stew using coconut milk. It will include steaming potatoes, broccoli, cabbage, beans and carrots or any other vegetable of your choice. Stir them in coconut milk with added herbs and spices.
- Experience the ingenuity of South Indian delicacies using coconut milk with recipes like semiya payasam (vermicelli pudding), nariyal ki kheer (coconut pudding), mongo kheer (mango pudding) and rice pudding.
- You can enjoy making kefir from coconut milk as a probiotic drink that everyone needs. Purchase a kefir starter culture pack and add one sachet of the culture to 0.5–1 litre of coconut milk in a glass or plastic jar. The volume will depend on the size of the packet. Stir the mixture gently and then close the lid of the container. Allow it to rest and culture at room temperature for 12–18 hours. Refrigerate it before drinking for a sense of delight and fulfillment.

Note: Both coconut kernel and its water serve as a healthy alternative to gain body mass if you are underweight as they contain plenty of calories.

3. CANTALOUPE MELON AND WATERMELON

Exceptionally high in water content (90 per cent), cantaloupe melons and watermelons taste sweet and have a soft texture. They impart a feeling of fullness when consumed before a meal. Don't be tricked by their sweetness for these fruits offer the least amount of calories.

Essential features and benefits

- They keep you well hydrated and help to replenish depleted electrolytes.
- They are packed with dietary fibre, facilitate weight loss and improve gut health.
- They treat indigestion and promote cardiac health.
- Loaded with multiple types of Vitamin B and other antioxidants, they help in reducing the risk of cancers and prevent memory loss due to aging.
- Both the fruits serve as a rich source of Vitamin C. A cupful of watermelon offers 25 per cent of the required daily value of Vitamin C, whereas the same amount of cantaloupe melon completely meets the requirement.
- They carry plenty of Vitamin A, promote good vision, boost immunity and increase the number of healthy red blood cells.

Note: Do not shy away from trying other varieties of melons like muskmelon and honeydew melon. They offer similar benefits.

Savour the sweet and refreshing flavour of melons

- Consume them as raw fruits either one hour before or after the meal.
- Include them in your fruit salads.
- Make a delightful watermelon juice to beat the scorching summer heat.
- Prepare a smoothie using cantaloupes, Greek yogurt and some jaggery powder.
- You can combine melon with basil, hard cheese, onions, red wine vinegar and olives for a sweet and savoury salad, the recipe for which you can find on the internet.

4. PEACHES

Though peaches too taste sweet, they offer low amounts of calories. They belong to the family of apricots, cherries and almonds, imparting an array of health benefits ranging from improving digestive health to enhancing skin tone.

Essential features and benefits

- It is loaded with a high content of water and Vitamin C, keeping the skin hydrated, improving the skin elasticity and protecting it from sun damage, imparting a natural glow to your skin.
- It helps treat indigestion and promote cardiac health.
- It carries a blend of antioxidants, reducing the risk of cancers and other chronic ailments by reversing inflammation and oxidative damage.
- Beta-carotene is a bioactive compound which, when consumed, gets converted into Vitamin A inside the body.

Peaches have plenty of naturally occurring Vitamin A as well as beta-carotene, promoting vision health, boosting immunity and increasing the number of healthy red blood cells.

- Having one of the lowest glycemic load, peaches add a sweet taste to the life of a diabetic patient.
- They have been shown to inhibit the release of histamine inside the bloodstream, indicating that they might help in reducing symptoms of allergy. Histamines are the chemicals that our immune system releases when our body is exposed to an allergen.

Make the most of this versatile fruit

- Consume them raw or whip them into smoothies.
- Add them to your oatmeal or eat them with yogurt and berries.
- Include them as an ingredient in making purée for sauces or fruit pudding.
- Use them while making a pie and other desserts.
- Peaches can be grilled and added to garden salads, turned into salsa or slivered into slaw.

5. KIWI

Kiwi is a small fruit with green flesh packed with plenty of health benefits. Along with a sweet and tangy flesh that gives it a characteristic flavour, kiwi also has edible black seeds.

Essential features and benefits

- One average-sized kiwi can nearly meet the complete daily requirement of Vitamin C. It is proven that kiwis have beneficial effects on lung function and improve airflow in asthmatic patients.
- It is one of the very few fruits that can actually help in preventing kidney stones from developing.
- It increases the number of blood platelets, making it an essential superfood for someone suffering from typhoid, malaria or dengue.
- It is packed with dietary fibre along with an enzyme called actinidin that not only improves digestion but also assists in efficient breakdown and metabolism of proteins.
- It enables the small intestines to retain water more effectively, resulting in better stool consistency and prevention of constipation.
- Loaded with potent antioxidants, it helps prevent and fight against oxidative stress, thereby reducing the likelihood of getting cancer.
- Regular consumption of kiwis can not only prevent from developing high blood pressure but also treat your existing hypertension.
- Kiwis help boost skin elasticity and reduce wrinkles.

Include kiwis in your diet arsenal

- Consume them raw or with yogurt.
- Toss them in your fruit salads for a sharp taste.
- Blend them with other fruits to make a flavoursome smoothie.
- Add sliced kiwis to your oatmeal or cereal-based recipe.

6. POMEGRANATES

Pomegranates are bright, red-coloured fruits that are botanically categorized as a berry. The skin of a pomegranate is thick and inedible. The edible part of a pomegranate are the hundreds of seeds inside which are red, juicy and have a sweet covering (referred to as an aril).

Essential features and benefits

- Pomegranates are laden with potent antioxidants, exhibiting impressive anti-inflammatory properties, which have proven beneficial in preventing as well as treating two of the most common cancers—breast and prostate.
- It significantly helps in managing blood pressure and reduces the risk of stroke.
- It contains many anti-diabetes compounds that improve insulin sensitivity, thereby preventing and even reversing the progression of diabetes.
- Its anti-inflammatory effects can also help in fighting arthritis and joint pain.
- When consumed in the form of juice, it has shown to significantly lower the levels of LDL (bad) cholesterol and triglycerides, thereby improving cardiac health and reducing the risk of a heart attack.
- It also helps in treating erectile dysfunction to some extent.

Sprinkle it all

- Satiate your evening hunger pangs with a bowl of pomegranates.
- Include them in your fruit salad.

- Sprinkle pomegranates on top of yogurt, oatmeal, custard, or smoothies.
- Incorporate them as fillings in milk-based desserts and home-made fruit puddings.
- Kick-start your mornings with fresh fruit-veggie salad, tossing pomegranate seeds into cooked and roasted sweet potatoes and brussels sprouts.
- Enjoy some pomegranate juice.

7. SINGHARA (WATER CHESTNUT)

Water chestnut is a unique seasonal fruit that grows in marshy areas, underwater and in the mud. Singhara tastes mildly sweet and has a crunchy texture. In India, it is popular during the times of Navaratri as people often fast, eating only fruits. Since water chestnut is a fruit, its flour is used to make rotis.

Essential features and benefits

- It contains plenty of water and dietary fibre content, which imparts a sensation of fullness and assists in weight loss.
- It carries a blend of antioxidants, reducing the risk of cancers and other chronic ailments by reversing inflammation and oxidative stress.
- It is an excellent source of potassium, aiding in regulating blood pressure, thereby reducing the risk of heart diseases.
- The blend of copper and manganese improves bone health, significantly reducing the risk of osteoporosis.

Can be enjoyed raw or cooked

- The crispy white flesh of water chestnut can be enjoyed raw or cooked and are a common addition to Asian dishes such as stir-fries, curries and salads.
- Include it as an ingredient in home-made pickles.
- Use chestnut flour to make chapattis as a healthier substitute for refined wheat flour, which is especially beneficial for diabetic patients.
- You can also use the flour for making water chestnut cake as a dessert with lesser calories.
- Appreciate the goodness of boiled or steamed water chestnuts by consuming them with amle ki chutney including mint and coriander leaves.
- Incorporate them as an ingredient in your sautéed or steamed vegetables and rice recipes.
- Peel, slice or grate them to include them into omelettes, curries, salads, etc.

MOVING ON FROM STRAWBERRIES

You must have heard a lot about strawberries and their health benefits, which indeed are true. In fact, strawberries are one of the healthiest fruits with the least amount of calories. However, they are quite expensive and not readily available with local fruit vendors. They are also hard to get at a quality grocery store.

If you rewind your memories, going to a supermarket, how many times have you actually ever seen strawberries kept on a shelf? And if you have seen them, how many times have you bought these fresh delicacies? Not too times, I suppose, the main reason being their cost and, of course, a general lack of knowledge about them. We do not associate ourselves with eating raw strawberries because of their low visibility and availability. Additionally, we prefer consuming them as an added flavour in cookies, candies and ice creams, so much so that we do not find it necessary to purchase them in their raw form.

But all that is about strawberries.

What about other the berries that are indigenous, readily available in the Indian market, and are much cheaper to buy, and more importantly, are as delicious and healthy as strawberries? Have you ever considered purchasing or knowing about them? They make up a large family.

If you haven't thought about them yet, it's high time you did.

8. RASBHARI (CAPE GOOSEBERRY)

Cape gooseberries, commonly referred to as rasbhari in India, are small orange-pink fruits belonging to the family of berries. They are grown as perennial fruits in the warm and tropical regions of India and are available in the markets across all seasons.

Essential features and benefits

- It contains a high amount of calcium and phosphorus along with pectin, which helps the body absorb them, thus promoting bone strength.
- It regulates blood pressure and lowers LDL (bad) cholesterol level, thereby improving cardiac health.
- It is packed with vitamins A and C, which assist in enhancing immunity and promoting vision health.

- It contains a blend of anti-inflammatory and antioxidants that help to resolve inflammation and treat the symptoms of asthma.
- Exhibiting strong antiviral properties, it guards against common flu and cold.

Add some juicy delight to your diet

- Consume them fresh and raw as a healthy snack.
- Toss them in a fruit salad.
- Have them with your oatmeal and yogurt for a wholesome breakfast.
- Use them as toppings in desserts or puddings.

DID YOU KNOW?

- Cape gooseberries serve as a powerhouse of more antioxidants than pomegranates, apples and broccoli.
- They also contain plenty of Vitamin C, more than what is found in lemon.

9. AMLA (INDIAN GOOSEBERRY)

Amla is a translucent green fruit that is packed with a plethora of nutrients, having the capability of protecting us from countless ailments, be it common cold, cancer or infertility. The name of the fruit originates from a Sanskrit word 'amlaki', that translates to 'nectar of life'.

Used since the ancient times, the name of the divine supplement itself highlights how significant it had been during those days. And now, science has proved that all of those indicated benefits were indeed correct.

Physicians, practicing naturopathy and following Ayurveda, claim that amla can help balance the three doshas (kapha, vata, pitta) in the body, eliminating the underlying cause of many diseases.

Essential features and benefits

- It exhibits powerful anti-inflammatory properties, repairing tissue damage and reducing the risk of cardiovascular disorders by half.
- Owing to its anti-inflammatory effects, amla also provides relief from arthritis-related joint aches.
- It reduces LDL (bad) cholesterol while keeping HDL (good) cholesterol level stable.
- It is loaded with potent antioxidants, preventing the growth of tumour cells and reducing the risk of cancer.
- It burns excessive fat, aiding in weight loss.
- It is packed with Vitamin C and thus boosts immunity.
- The best anti-aging fruit, it helps one get wrinkle-free, healthy and glowing skin.
- It serves as a blood purifier and a detoxifying agent, removing toxins from the gut.
- It stimulates insulin production, reducing the blood glucose level, thereby effective in treating Type 2 diabetes.
- Presence of carotene makes it an excellent condiment for improving vision and overall eye health.

Let amla be your medicine

The benefits mentioned above prove that amla is a potent nature's grace to us to aid in combating against most of our everyday health woes. As healthy as amla is, it is also easy to use and consume.

- Make the most out of amla by drinking its fresh juice, including ginger, coriander leaves, mint and a dash of honey in it. Dilute the juice with water according to your taste and drink it first thing in the morning for effective blood purification.
- Mix amla juice with jamun (Indian blackberry) and karela (bitter gourd) juice to manage and treat diabetes in the most efficient manner possible.
- Amla juice, in combination with aloe vera juice, does wonders for your heart as it brings down both triglyceride and LDL (bad) cholesterol level.
- For better eyesight, take the juice at bedtime.
- Without mixing any other ingredient, dilute the unadulterated juice in half a cup of lukewarm water and gargle with it to attain immaculate oral health.
- Boost your gut health by incorporating amle ka achaar (pickle) in your meals.
- Sprinkle grated amla on top of your fruit salad.
- Prepare amle ki chutney with fennel, mint and coriander or brahmi leaves for adding zesty flavours that will complement almost anything you eat.

DID YOU KNOW?

- Amla has more Vitamin C than an orange.
- It is loaded with twice the antioxidant power of acai berry and around 17 times that of a pomegranate.

10. JAMUN (JAVA PLUM)

Jamun, aka black plum or java plum, is a summer fruit with a tart flavour, which is associated with many health and medicinal benefits. Also known as Indian blackberry, the densely nutritious fruit is known to relieve stomach pain and flatulence. Jamun vinegar is beneficial for those who have urine retention issues and enlarged spleen.

Essential features and benefits

- Diuretic in nature, it flushes toxins out of the kidneys, promoting kidney health.
- It serves as a tonic to increase libido.
- It is a rich source of potassium and keeps blood pressure in check.
- It carries a stimulating blend of anti-inflammatory and antioxidants like anthocyanin, minimizing the risk of liver disease, preventing the growth of tumour cells and reducing the risk of cancer.
- It improves insulin sensitivity, converts starch into energy, thereby preventing and even reversing the progression of diabetes.
- Packed with an adequate amount of iron, it increases the haemoglobin count and acts as a blood purifying agent.
- Loads of Vitamin C in jamun helps in treating scurvy and boosts immunity.
- It treats GI-related disorders like diarrhoea, stomach pain, flatulence and prevents the development of peptic ulcers.
- It provides strength to teeth and gum promoting oral health.

Pickle them or eat as dessert

- Consume them fresh and raw or make a juice out of them.
- Include them in a fruit-veggie salad, along with mango, cucumber, tomato and cabbage with a luscious dressing of virgin olive oil, lemon and a pinch of salt.
- You can incorporate them in desserts for an astringent flavour.
- Adding jamun in pickles is the best way to use them.
- Try a frozen yogurt recipe using java plums.

DID YOU KNOW?

- Jamun seeds are equally healthy. You can have jamun seeds in a powdered form.
- After you have consumed the flesh of the java plum, do not discard the seeds. Keep them in a plate and let them dry naturally.
- When they have dried well, crush them and grind them using a mixer-grinder to make their powder.

---

11. BER (INDIAN JUJUBE)

Jujube or ber, as we Indians call it, is a fruit with a mildly tart and sweet taste, having a slightly hard texture. There are different varieties and many cultivars of ber. While some ripen in October, others may ripe in February, March or April depending upon their variety and where they are grown.

These berries can range from being brown to purple-black in colour. It is perhaps the only indigenous berry that sells at slightly high rates in India. But jujubes impart mind-boggling health benefits, which make them totally worth it.

Essential features and benefits

- It exhibits soothing effect on the entire nervous system, treating anxiety and helping you have a better and sound sleep.
- A high quantum of fibre in jujubes helps to improve digestion, provides relief from constipation and regulates bowel movements.
- Jujubes have high contents of essential minerals and antioxidants, reducing the risk of many chronic ailments.
- Particularly rich in Vitamin C, it helps improve skin tone and boosts immunity.
- It is loaded with high potassium, improving blood circulation and easing down blood pressure.
- It contains significant amounts of calcium, iron and phosphorus, thus promoting bone strength. It also helps prevent and reverse the onset of osteoporosis.

Add a handful of health while you snack

- Include fresh jujube in your evening snacks and consume them raw.
- Use smashed jujube, adding them to a fruit-veggie salad along with jaggery powder, fresh coriander leaves, chopped green chillies and salt to taste.
- Prepare ber ki chutney, which will be complimenting your traditional meals.
- Another well-known use of ber is in traditional berry pickles with cumin, jaggery, rock salt and green chilies.
- Drink fresh ber juice to replenish your body with essential nutrients. Blend the berries well with some sugar and cold water in a juicer-mixer to obtain the pulp—fleshy residues

of ber. Mash the mix on a sieve to extract the entire juice in a container below.

12. SHEHTOOT (MULBERRY)

Mulberries are the sweet berries grown under varied climatic conditions ranging from temperate to tropical. These delicate berries come in black and red colours. They are a low-calorie food, offering high water content. Mulberries in India are available for a short period twice a year—first from March to May and then from October to November.

Essential features and benefits

- Mulberries are rich in essential nutrients like iron, Vitamin C and potassium, offering a plethora of health benefits. These include, but are not limited to, increasing haemoglobin count, improving blood circulation, boosting immunity, easing down blood pressure, etc.
- It serves as a powerhouse of potent antioxidants, which helps in repairing tissue damage, cutting the risk of cardiovascular disorders significantly, guarding against chronic ailments like cancer, cardiovascular disorders, etc.
- It brings down LDL (bad) cholesterol levels.
- It protects against diabetes by inhibiting the enzyme that breaks down carbs into simple sugars, thereby controlling blood sugar levels from spiking.
- It helps in alleviating symptoms of constipation, bloating and abdominal cramping.
- It exhibits anti-aging properties, promoting youthfulness and glowing skin.

Use as snack or hair product

- Consume them fresh and raw as a healthy snacking option.
- Toss them in a bowl of fruit or vegetable salad for a wholesome meal.
- Consume mulberry juice regularly to reap maximum benefits.
- Apart from making it part of your diet, you can also apply mulberry juice to your hair to prevent premature graying as it aids in the production of melanin in your hair.

COMPLIMENTS FROM OTHER INDIGENOUS FORGOTTEN BERRIES AND FRUITS

Moving on from commonly-known berries, let's delve into discussing the health benefits of other berries and fruits that have their roots in India. These indigenous eatables were once popular among us, but are now seldom consumed at our homes in their raw state. Their usage has become limited to being sold as refreshment drinks at small kiosks.

1. Karonda (carissa carandas)

Another unique and indigenous, but not so well-known berry is karonda. Believed to be originating from the Himalayas, it is a small fruit with vibrant whitish-pink color, exhibiting a sweet-and-sour taste.

Essential features and benefits

- Karondas are rich in carotenoids, which are antioxidants that boost your immunity and promote health of eyes, skin and hair. Carotenoids are also responsible for imparting pinkish/reddish color to karondas.

- The fruit is packed with iron and Vitamin C. It also inhibits the excessive secretion of bile, promoting liver health. It is particularly useful to prevent and treat symptoms of diarrhoea.

Karonde ki chutney

Prepare lip-smacking karonde ki chutney by mixing and grinding 1 cup of finely chopped coriander leaves and a few green chilies with a bowl of karondas, chopped garlic, a pinch of asafoetida, ½ teaspoon of cumin seeds and salt to taste. The chutney tastes the the best with arbi ki sabzi, though you can serve it with any other vegetable as well.

Other uses

You can also use unripe karonda as an ingredient in making spicy pickles and traditional Indian curries. It can be used as a substitute for aamchoor (mango powder) to impart unique tanginess, which you cannot get from tomatoes or other flavouring food.

2. Phalsa

Another less popular, but high in nutritious quality, phalsa is a purple-coloured fruit that has a distinctive sweet and sour taste. Their short cultivation season (May–June) and the shelf life of only a couple of days makes them scarcely available in the market.

Essential features and benefits

- Though it is scarcely available in the market, its health benefits make it worthy to be consumed as much as possible.
- It contains rare phytochemicals as antioxidants, which are unique to purple-coloured fruits, exhibiting anti-inflammatory properties.
- It promotes cardiac health and is helpful in treating problems of the urinary tract.
- It helps in stabilizing the blood sugar levels among diabetics.
- It comes loaded with calcium, iron, phosphorus and vitamins B, C and A.
- The Ayurveda contains mentions of phalsa for imparting cooling sensation during summers.

From the vault of our memories

The readers, those who are of my generation from the '80s and '90s, would remember how we would eagerly wait for the street vendor to give out a call, '*kaale kaale phalse, sherbet wale phalse!* (black black phalsa, sweet-tasting phalsa!)' And we would either run or ask our mothers to get them for us.

The super-cool summer drink: Phalsa sherbet

Extract the pulp from phalsa using a blender and strain them through a sieve. Add cold water, jaggery powder, ¼ teaspoon each of black salt and roasted cumin seeds powder. A quarter kilogram of phalsa would make about 4–6 glasses of juice.

3. Kokum (Garcinia indica)

Native to the Konkan coast, kokum has been traditionally used in Goa and Maharashtra for making chutney and sherbet. Since the fruit is a member of the *garcinia* genus, it serves as a potent fat cutter and helps in losing weight and treating obesity.

Essential features and benefits

- It is known for treating acidity, digestive discomfort and bloating.
- It carries potent antioxidants, combating oxidative stress.
- It reduces cholesterol levels, promoting cardiac health.
- A glass of kokum sherbet can impart a satisfying cooling sensation, beating the scorching summer heat.

Savor the taste of Konkan

- Do not complete your Goa trip without having a couple of glasses of kokum juice.
- Include the ingredient in making traditional dishes of Maharashtra, Goa and Gujarat.
- People use it as a preferred substitute to tamarind as it imparts a unique sweet and sour taste as well as a rich colour and distinct aroma to the dish.
- Serve the tangy and zesty kokum chutney with your traditional recipes.

4. Bael fruit (stone apple)

Native to India, bael fruits have hard woody exterior enriched with aromatic pulp inside. Ayurveda regards bael as a significant herb with certain medicinal properties describing it as anti-inflammatory and useful in treating hemorrhoids. The fruit serves as a natural coolant, and its drink can offer you an unparalleled and unmatched freshness that no other beverage can provide.

Essential features and benefits

- It is packed with antioxidants that can be beneficial in treating gastric ulcers, heart and liver ailments.
- It exhibits natural laxative properties, preventing constipation and promoting overall digestive health.
- It imparts an instant cooling sensation.
- It is extremely nutritious, replenishing the body with an abundance of vitamins C and A, potassium, iron and calcium.
- It exhibits potent anti-bacterial and anti-fungal properties, promoting gut health.

Bael sherbet

Bael sherbet provides instant energy quenching your thirst.

Crack-open the fruit and scoop out the pulp from within. Mix the pulp well with water and strain it to remove any solid impurities. Add chilled water, whole ground cardamom powder, jaggery and black salt to the mixture. And enjoy the robust drink! But do not hesitate to consume the raw pulp as well.

11

NUTS AND SEEDS

Having learned about fruits, vegetables, grains, herbs and spices, it's time to shift our focus towards nuts and seeds, which impart greater goodness of health. They are often mentioned together because of the similar nutrient profiles they carry. The category of nuts comprises almonds, cashews, pistachios and walnuts. Botanically, peanuts are part of the family of legumes but often considered as nuts due to similar characteristics. The most commonly consumed seeds include pumpkin seeds, flax seeds, sesame seeds, chia seeds, melon seeds and sunflower seeds.

Nuts and seeds are often used for snacking, munching, or garnishing main-course meals. However, one should not underestimate the health benefits that a single ounce of these little gems can offer. Rich in healthy fats, both nuts and seeds offer significant benefits in supporting weight loss and protecting against chronic ailments like diabetes and cardiac disorders. Furthermore, they carry zero amount of trans-fat, thereby keeping the levels of triglycerides under check.

The most unique attribute of nuts and seeds is that they are extremely dense in micronutrients. Hence, even a limited amount of their consumption goes a long way in meeting the deficiencies of essential nutrients.

They are readily available in the market. People might say

that some of these nuts and seeds, especially almonds, pistachios and chia seeds are expensive. But if you consider the amount you will be consuming in a day, you will realize that you will not need to buy a bag full of them. You can purchase them in moderate amounts and consume them in a couple of months. Just pick and choose your favorite nuts and seeds according to your taste and requirements and enjoy the crunch.

BREAKING OPEN NUTS AND THEIR MYTHS FOR HEALTH REVELATIONS

We look at nuts as mere snacks that satiate our cravings. But it is a fact that nuts are an excellent source of protein, serving as a supplement for energy and source for building muscle tissues. It is true that nuts and raisins are high-calorie foods. However, their GL is quite low (less than five), implying that they do not stimulate a spike in blood sugar levels.

Another myth that stops people from consuming nuts regularly is that they cause weight gain because they are high in cholesterol and fats. But the truth is far from it as the popular saying goes 'A half-truth is much worse than a lie.' All the foods falling under the category of nuts, along with peanuts, help to raise HDL (good) cholesterol and reduce the levels of LDL (bad) cholesterol and triglycerides, promoting cardiac and liver health. Nuts have fats in the form of omega-3, omega-6 and other medium chain triglycerides, which are the healthiest form of fats.

Also, nuts, of any type, carry plenty of dietary fibre. This combination of proteins, healthy fats and fibre gives them a quality of supporting and maintaining weight loss. This blend of macronutrients also makes them one of the favorite foods of good bacteria residing inside the gut, contributing to their growth and improving gut health.

A Word of Caution

High in calories, nuts are not supposed to be taken as a proper meal but natural supplements in a limited amount. They significantly fulfill the recommended daily value (RDV) of various micronutrients and dietary fibre. Hence, one should consider consuming them daily as a much healthier alternate to eating chips and fast food. Do not deprive yourself of reaping benefits of these health gems. Just remember when to put a stop.

1. Walnuts

Walnuts are small-sized and irregularly shaped single-seeded stone fruits that grow on walnut tree. Appearing similar to the neural network of the human brain, walnuts are indeed the most potent ingredient that enhances brain functioning and promotes cognitive health.

Essential features and benefits

- They promote neuronal and brain health.
- They contain healthy fats and decent amounts of dietary fibre, supporting weight loss and improving gut health.
- They are rich in Vitamin E, which acts as a strong antioxidant and help in combating oxidative damage inside the body.
- They are loaded with certain bioactive compounds that are anti-inflammatory and known to reduce risk of breast and prostate cancers. However, extensive human studies are needed to make a stronger claim.
- They help lower blood pressure and reduce the risk of Type 2 diabetes.
- A few studies have shown that walnuts improve sperm

count and vitality, thus are instrumental in promoting reproductive health in males.[51] [52]

> **DID YOU KNOW?**
>
> • Walnuts contain the highest amount of omega-3 amongst nuts, help enhance cardiac health and reduce the risk of cardiovascular disease.

2. Almonds

Almonds are off-white-coloured nuts covered in a brown-coloured skin. They are derived from almond trees, which are believed to be one of the oldest trees cultivated, approximately 19,000 years ago, even before millets.[53] Crunchy in texture and rich in nutrition, almonds have served as a snack satiating cravings and managing appetite.

Essential qualities and benefits

• It is the second most potent ingredient after walnuts in enhancing brain functioning and promoting cognitive health.

---

[51] Albert Salas-Huetos and Jordi Salas-Salvado, 'Tree nuts for erectile dysfunction and male infertility: A natural drug?', *Nutfruit Magazine*, 2016, p: 48–49.

[52] Albert Salas-Huetos, Rocío Moraleda, Simona Giardina, et al., 'Effect of nut consumption on semen quality and functionality in healthy men consuming a Western-style diet: a randomized controlled trial', *The American Journal of Clinical Nutrition*, Vol. 108, Issue 5, November 2018, p: 953–62.

[53] Gargi Sharma, 'Why Soaked Almonds Are Better Than Raw Almonds', *NDTV Food*, 28 October 2021, https://food.ndtv.com/opinions/why-soaked-almonds-are-better-than-raw-almonds-726909. Accessed on 20 December 2021.

- It is packed with dietary fibre and healthy fats, facilitating in weight loss and improving gut health.
- Eating almonds regularly have been found to be associated with a low risk of developing breast cancer.
- Almonds carry a potent blend of antioxidants including Vitamin E and flavonoids, promoting cardiac health and diminishing the risk of Alzheimer's.
- The brown skin of almonds also contains antioxidants, which is why they should be consumed with their skin intact. Eat them early in the morning after having soaked them overnight in water.
- They serve as a rich source of magnesium, controlling blood sugar levels.
- Almonds also carry a decent amount of manganese, copper, protein, phosphorus and zinc, all of which contribute to bone health.
- They are like natural Vitamin B complex containing 25 per cent of the RDV of Vitamin B2, along with decent amounts of vitamins B3 and B1 and traces of vitamins B9, B5 and B6.

DID YOU KNOW?

- A fistful of almonds can meet about 12–15 per cent of your daily protein needs.
- Almonds are one of the richest sources of Vitamin E, providing about 40–45 per cent of RDV from one ounce (28 g).

---

3. Cashew Nut

Native to Brazil, cashews were brought to India by various traders over the years. Cashews have a great shelf life if stored properly. Widely regarded throughout the world for their delicate flavour, they exhibit extraordinary health benefits.

Essential features and benefits

- They contain a strong antioxidant pigment called zeaxanthin, which is directly and readily absorbed by our retina, protecting our eyes from various infections.
- Packed with dietary fibre, they facilitate weight loss and improve gut health.
- Cashews are a great source of zinc and selenium, both of which are significant in boosting immunity, improving brain functioning and promoting cognitive health, thereby reducing the risk of Alzheimer's. Selenium deficiency has been strongly associated with increased risk of cancer and hypothyroidism (as selenium is critical for the proper functioning of the thyroid gland).
- They carry decent amounts of vitamins E and K, both of which serve as antioxidants, helping combat oxidative damage at multiple levels.

DID YOU KNOW?

- Regularly eating cashews can reduce the risk of developing gallstones by up to 25 per cent.
- One ounce of cashews can meet your entire requirement of daily intake of copper, improving blood count, promoting bone health and preventing anaemia. It becomes even more significant, given the fact that not many other foods offer enough copper, which is one of the most essential micronutrients.

4. Pistachios

Originated from the Middle East, pistachios were grown there for thousands of years before getting transported worldwide. They are also referred to in the Old Testament of the Bible. Greenish in color, these slightly sweet and earthy flavoured nuts offer a nutritious value matching its high price.

Pistachios are the extraordinary exception among nuts as they carry fewer calories and can be consumed in moderate amounts.

Essential features and benefits

- Pistachios are one of the richest sources of vitamins B6 and B1, both of which are crucial in maintaining neural and mental health.
- They are also the most prolific source of lutein and zeaxanthin, both of which are powerful antioxidants promoting ocular health and protecting our eyes against various infections and age-related macular degeneration.
- They carry decent amounts of iron, stimulating the formation of haemoglobin.
- A few studies have reported better management of blood sugars with regular consumption of pistachios, indicating that it cannot only .prevent but also reverse diabetes.[54][55]

---

[54]Pablo Hernández-Alonso, Jordi Salas-Salvadó, Mònica Baldrich-Mora, Martí Juanola-Falgarona, Mònica Bulló 3, 'Beneficial Effect of Pistachio Consumption on Glucose Metabolism, Insulin Resistance, Inflammation, and Related Metabolic Risk Markers: A Randomized Clinical Trial', *Diabetes Care*, 37(11): 2014, p: 3098-3105.

[55]Mahmoud Parham, Saeide Heidari, Ashraf Khorramirad, Mohammad Hozoori, Fatemeh Hosseinzadeh, Lida Bakhtyari, Jamshid Vafaeimanesh,

- Pistachios stimulate and promote better vasodilation (widening of blood vessels) and overall health of blood vessels, regulating blood pressure effectively.
- With improved vasodilation, they can treat erectile dysfunction as well.

DID YOU KNOW?

Pistachios serve as an extraordinary source of various micronutrients. In terms of RDV, they offer about 40 per cent copper, 25 per cent Vitamin B6, 20 per cent Vitamin B1, 15 per cent magnesium and 10 per cent each of magnesium and phosphorus. It implies that pistachios are extremely useful in promoting cardiac, bone, nervous and mental health. They are also critical in improving cognitive functioning. Furthermore, regular consumption of pistachios can improve blood count and prevent anaemia.

5. Peanuts

Botanically, peanuts are legumes that are related to beans and lentils. They are not nuts but regarded as such due to a similar nutrient profile and other physical characteristics. Extremely crunchy and delicious, they are off-white in colour and covered under a vibrant reddish-brown skin.

There are contrary views about peanut skin, indicating its benefits as well as some harmful traits. So, it's better you eat them after after peeling off their skin. The outer coat offers

'Effects of pistachio Nut Supplementation on Blood Glucose in Patients With Type 2 Diabetes: A Randomized Crossover Trial', *Review of Diabetic Studies*, 11(2), 2014, p: 190–6.

some antioxidants, similar types of which are also available through the peanut itself and other nuts, fruits and vegetables. So, you can get plenty of those antioxidants one way or the other.

Often consumed raw or roasted, peanuts have also found their way to our kitchen in the form of peanut butter and groundnut oil. Peanut butter is added in shakes and smoothies and applied over toast, whereas groundnut oil can be used for cooking. One can gain similar nutritional benefits as peanuts from both butter and oil. However, use the butter in limited amounts (not more than 2 teaspoons) as it is rich in calories. Also, make sure to purchase the cold-pressed version of the oil and not the one that's refined.

Essential features and benefits

- They carry plant-based protein and healthy fats in abundance, improving core strength and promoting gut health.
- They are loaded with a potent blend of antioxidants, reducing the risk of cancer and protecting the liver from oxidative damage.
- They serve as an excellent source of B vitamins, boosting metabolism and cellular signalling, improving mental, cognitive and neural health and repairing DNA damage.

Note: Binge eating salted/packed peanuts can definitely impact your heart health adversely because of high sodium content that can raise your blood pressure and affect kidneys in the long run.

DID YOU KNOW?

An ounce of peanuts (a handful of them) can go a long way in meeting your body's daily requirement of copper, manganese, phosphorus, magnesium and vitamins B1, B7, B9 and E. It implies that peanuts are extremely useful in promoting cardiac, bone, neural, neuronal and mental health. They are also critical in improving cognitive functioning. Furthermore, regular consumption of peanuts can help to improve blood count and prevent anaemia.

Peanuts contain more amount of protein than any other nuts.

6. Munakka

Moving on from crunchy and hard texture nuts, we take a look at soft and sweet munakka that imparts coolness in the body. Munakka or dried grape is a raisin that has found its use in traditional Indian medicine and is commonly recommended as part of a diet to those recovering from chronic illness. Munakka can either be taken in dried form or soaked overnight to improve digestion and treat symptoms of acidity.

Munakka is slightly different from kishmish in physical appearance in the sense that it is significantly larger in size and darker in color. Also, it has multiple seeds, whereas kishmish mostly comes seedless.

Both munakka and kishmish have a similar nutrient profile, but the latter has an additional tang in it that produces acidity inside the body, which might cause some uncomfortable gastric symptoms, including reflux. Additionally, munakka contains more iron and magnesium than its kishmish.

Essential features and benefits

- Munakka exhibits laxative and cooling attributes, which are useful for managing constipation and acidity, respectively.
- It also imparts soothing and cough suppressant properties, efficient in treating dry cough and respiratory tract inflammation.
- It serves as an excellent source of iron and magnesium, improving haemoglobin count, regulating blood pressure, and promoting cognitive, mental, muscle and bone health.
- It stimulates the production of nitric oxide in the blood, improving vasodilation and blood vessels health, thereby treating high blood pressure.
- It carries a powerful blend of antioxidants that helps to inhibit the growth of tumour cells and prevents certain types of cancer like colon cancer.
- Its antioxidants and other nutrients are good for ocular health and protect your eyes from glaucoma, night blindness, cataract, etc.

Nuts and raisins are increasingly being used over chips as favorite snacks due to their pleasant taste and their ability to satiate hunger, that too in their natural form. However, we need to win over our tendency to purchase packed foods and stop buying a salted version of these nuts.

A small packet of salted nuts might seem cheap, but if you extrapolate the quantity to half kilogram, you will realize you're paying a much higher price than what you would have paid had you purchased raw nuts.

Crack open nuts and add raisins for wholesome goodness

- Garnish halwa, kheer, puddings and cakes with almonds,

munakka, cashews and pistachios.

- Peanuts are tasty, easy-to-eat options for munching while working or for having as snacks with evening tea. Grab a fistful of almonds, cashews, pistachios and walnuts along with munakka and carry them to your workplace in a small box.
- Whenever you feel peckish in between meals or feel like snacking, grab a handful of raw or dry roasted nuts for a crunchy delight instead of eating biscuits or fruit cake.
- You can sprinkle nuts and raisins over smoothies, shakes, oatmeal or yogurt. You can also blend them while making shakes and beverages.
- Serve them atop leafy vegetable or fruit salads.
- Chop them and add them to your wraps or sandwiches.
- Give your kids five to six pieces of almonds and walnuts early in the morning before they go to school to help boost their brain functioning.
- Give a twist of taste to walnuts by caramelizing them with jaggery.
- Use roasted and chopped nuts in pasta, biryani and dry vegetables.
- Consume munakka on an empty stomach early in the morning after keeping it soaked in water overnight to boost iron levels, increase blood count and treat anaemia.
- Nuts and raisins serve as one of the best alternates for vegetarians to meet their requirements of protein, fat, copper, iron, zinc and B vitamins.

Note: It is healthiest to consume nuts in its raw form or when they are roasted dry. Avoid baking them in vegetable or seed oils.

Sonth ke ladoo with nuts and raisins

This is a magical remedy for treating general pain and

postpartum-related weakness.

Sonth ke laddu is a traditional recipe, specially prepared for new mothers for consumption post delivery. Ingredients like sonth (dry ginger powder), gond (tragacanth gum) and various nuts offer high protein and more than adequate supply of macronutrients. The potent blend of these super ingredients helps in repairing muscles and exhibits anti-inflammatory properties, thereby strengthening the body. In general, sonth ka ladoo has been proven to be beneficial in treating back pain and muscle weakness.

Ingredients

- ⅓ cup of sonth (ginger powder)
- 1¼ cup of jaggery
- ½ cup of ghee
- 1 cup of dry grated coconut
- ¾ cup of whole wheat flour
- ½ cup of raisins and chopped nuts, including almonds, pistachios, cashews
- ¼ cup of gond

Method

i.   Cut gond, almonds, cashews, pistachios and raisins into small pieces.
ii. Heat ½ cup of ghee and roast gond on a low-to-medium flame. After taking out the roasted gond, add whole wheat flour to the same hot ghee and roast it well until dark brown.
iii. Heat 2 teaspoons of ghee. Add sonth to it and roast it on a medium flame.
iv. Grind jaggery and heat the powder till it melts. Separately, grind the softened roasted gond.

v. Add roasted flour, sonth, nuts, raisins, gond and grated coconut to the melted jaggery and mix the ingredients well.

vi. Roll them into ladoos and appreciate its wholesome goodness by having one every day.

SOWING THE SEEDS OF GOOD HEALTH

One common attribute found in nuts of all types is that they come densely packed with fats, proteins, fibre and essential micronutrients. One or two ounces of nuts can suffice our daily nutrient needs. But what if you're told that there's a type of food with similar nutrient profile and is even more jam-packed with nutrients? Yes, you heard it right! And the answer is seeds, such as that of pumpkin, flax, sesame, sunflower, chia, etc.

It is logical for tiny seeds to have denser amounts of nutrients and serve as superfoods. After all, they have to germinate into an entire full-grown plant of the next generation, bearing fruits in future. So, they must contain all the nutrients required for their development.

Seeds are the powerhouse of proteins and dietary fibre and are packed with essential fatty acids, amino acids, minerals along with vitamins A, B, C and E. The affluent nutrient profile helps a great deal in strengthening one's immunity and warding off various chronic ailments. More importantly, they serve as one of the healthiest snacking options to satiate your hunger and keep you away from overeating unhealthy salted/sweetened bites with added preservatives and trans-fats.

Since the nutrients in the seeds are so densely packed, we don't have to eat a lot of them. One teaspoon of them can meet 5–15 per cent of RDV of various essential minerals and vitamins. In fact, one to 2 teaspoons of flaxseed or chia seeds can satisfy your entire RDV of omega-3 and dietary fibre. Nutritionists recommend that 2 teaspoons of these nutritional delights are enough. Keep boxes of various seeds on your kitchen shelf and select one of them to consume a particular day.

Let's explore the common attributes of these seeds and how they impart invaluable health benefits.

- Having extraordinarily low GL, seeds are extremely high in dietary fibre and quality protein. It makes them an excellent source for slow and sustainable release of energy and enables them to keep the blood sugars stabilized.
- They are rich in complex carbs, serving as a significant feed for good bacteria residing in the colon, enhancing the overall gut health.
- Seeds offer unbelievably large quantities of fibre and protein, imparting a feeling of fullness and satiety for longer periods, supporting weight loss and preventing as well as treating obesity.
- Seeds offer plenty of healthy and essential fatty acids like omega-3, promoting cardiac and liver health.
- Every type of seed improves insulin sensitivity, regulating blood sugar levels and not only preventing Type 2 diabetes but also reversing its progression.

ENJOY THE CRUNCH

- Seeds can be consumed raw, cooked with stew, or sprinkled over whole cereal meal, salads and soups as garnishing.
- You can dry-roast them and consume them as you would use raw seeds.

- Place them in a tray and keep it inside an oven pre-heated to 180 degrees Celsius for 10 minutes. Alternatively, you can toast them on a pre-heated pan until they start changing their colour and imparting a smoky flavour. Ensure that you do not burn them. If you're using an oven, keep monitoring them for colour change.
- Add roasted or raw seeds in kheer, halwa, ice creams and fruit puddings or sauté them to incorporate them in vegetable dishes.

Let us now look at the individual qualities of various kinds of seeds.

1. Alsi (flaxseeds)

Originating in the region of Mesopotamia, the flax plant became popular among Egyptians, who used it as medicine for treating GI-related issues. Hippocrates has mentioned in his writings about using flaxseeds to treat abdominal pains. But the major push in its popularity came in the eighth century, when King Charlemagne, also known as 'Charles the Great' passed laws requiring his subjects to consume flaxseeds as he strongly believed in its health benefits, which gave them the name *Linum usitatissimum* (in Latin), meaning 'the most useful'. Nowadays, flaxseeds, also known as linseeds, are emerging as one of the superfoods.

Essential features and benefits

- They serve as an excellent source of omega-3 and omega-6 essential fatty acids, promoting cardiac and liver health.
- Flaxseeds carry alpha-linolenic acid (ALA) in great amounts. ALA is a plant-based omega-3 fatty acid, which

is not only beneficial for the heart, brain and immunity but also essential for preventing thrombotic disease, cancer and male infertility. Regular intake of ALA has been linked to lowering the risk of stroke.

- ALA is an anti-inflammatory that comes in handy for treating symptoms of arthritis, joint pain and muscle stiffness. Because of carrying significant amounts of ALA, flaxseeds are now being used medicinally to treat and prevent auto-immune diseases like rheumatoid arthritis, Type 1 diabetes and systemic lupus.
- The seeds have high content of soluble and insoluble fibre, serving as a laxative and assisting in treating symptoms of constipation.
- They are absolutely gluten-free.
- They are extremely rich in manganese, magnesium, phosphorus and copper, promoting bone health, improving metabolism and improving blood count.
- They contain significant amounts of vitamins B6 and B9, promoting neural and mental health, preventing dementia, Alzheimer's and clinical depression.
- Flaxseeds are the richest source of lignans, a potent plant-based antioxidant, which enhances the longevity, helps relieving menopausal symptoms such as hot flashes, and reduces the risk of cancer, particularly that of breast and colon.

Store some for wholesome goodness

- Nutritionists recommend consuming 3 teaspoons (one ounce) of flaxseeds daily to reap maximum benefits out of them. Alternatively, you can try having 1–2 teaspoons of flaxseed oil.

- One needs to ground flaxseeds as it is difficult for our intestines to break down the tough outer shell of the whole seeds. You can purchase whole flaxseeds, grind them in a coffee grinder and store them in an airtight container.
- Ground seeds can then be added to your oatmeal or sprinkled over or blended in hot/cold cereals, yogurt, smoothies and soup.
- Drizzle flaxseed oil as a dressing on fruit and vegetable salad.
- Relive the traditions of North India by making alsi ki pinnia with added nuts and raisins, popular in the regions of Haryana and Punjab.

Versatile use of flaxseed water

- Use 3 teaspoons of whole flax seeds and soak them in a glass of warm water for 15–20 minutes.
- As the water turns opaque and slightly viscous, you can add this water removing the seeds to smoothies, soups or stews and make it part of your daily fluid intake.
- You can also use this water in the batter to prepare bread, cookies or other baked food.
- This fluid mix can be used as an egg substitute to prepare confectionery items. The water will retain its inherent beneficial attributes.

DID YOU KNOW?

For a Healthy Heart, Mind and Brain

Flaxseeds are the most abundant source of omega-3. One tablespoon of flaxseed can entirely fulfill your recommended daily intake of essential fatty acid.

Knitting the Fabric of Health with Dietary Fibre

One tablespoon of flax seeds contains 3 g fibre. Regular intake of flaxseeds can be a blessing for your gut health as it helps in slowing down your digestion rate. This results in more effective absorption of nutrients and improvement in the consistency of stools, helping in a thorough cleansing of the colon and gut, which can prevent as well as treat conditions like constipation and IBS.

Ingredients for jawasachi chutney (flaxseed chutney)

- 1 cup of flaxseeds
- 1 teaspoon of red chilli powder
- ¼ spoon of turmeric powder
- 1 teaspoon of coriander-cumin seeds powder
- Salt to taste
- 5–7 garlic cloves (optional)

Method

i.   Roast one cup of flaxseeds for five to seven minutes.

ii. Add roasted flaxseeds, 1 teaspoon of red chilli powder, ¼ teaspoon of whole turmeric powder, one teaspoon of coriander-cumin seeds powder and salt as per taste to the mixer-grinder.

iii. Grind the mixture well for two to three minutes.

iv. (Optional) After a round of grinding, you can then also add 5–7 cloves of garlic and blend them again. Your jawasachi chutney is ready!

v.   Serve the zesty chutney with traditional vegetable dishes or jowar ki roti.

2. Chia seeds

If you have regarded flaxseeds as the king of superfoods, then you might be in for a surprise. And the reason is chia seeds, giving a 'healthy' competition to flaxseeds. Chia seeds offer more dietary fibre, calcium, phosphorus, iron and selenium than flaxseeds.

Chia seeds are valued for their potential to supply sustainable energy. In fact, the name 'chia' originates from an ancient Mayan word meaning 'strength'.

Essential features and benefits

- Chia seeds are packed with antioxidants.
- Chia seeds have been associated with increased HDL cholesterol levels as well as reduced levels of triglycerides and LDL cholesterol.
- One ounce of chia seeds provides a significant percent of RDV of calcium, phosphorus, selenium, magnesium, manganese and iron, promoting bone, brain and thyroid health and preventing as well as reversing osteoporosis.
- They carry incredibly high amounts of fibre and complex carbs. Moreover, they are absolutely gluten-free.
- They are regarded as the most potent food that helps in treating chronic fatigue
- It has been clinically proven that chia seeds assist in significantly reducing and reversing chronic inflammation.
- They are efficient in detoxifying the GI tract, cleansing the gut and colon, facilitating excretion of toxins through bile and stool.

DID YOU KNOW?

Just 2 tablespoons of chia seeds can meet your daily requirement of omega-3 and omega-6.

Chia seeds are indisputably the most prolific source of dietary fiber and complex carbohydrates, offering approximately 12 g each of them for every ounce (28 g) consumed. It allows them to help in digestion and prevent bowel-related ailments (like constipation and bowel inflammation and irritability). Furthermore, it focuses on the growth of good bacteria inside the gut, promoting cardiac health, immunity, brain health and digestion.

Get some chia energy!

Chia seeds can be effortlessly incorporated in one's diet. You don't have to ground them like flax seeds and can use them as whole. Furthermore, they are bland in taste. So, you can add them to pretty much anything.

- Consume them raw or sprinkle them atop cereal, yogurt, oatmeal, smoothies, cold coffee, fruit salads, stewed vegetables or rice dishes.
- Use chia water as a substitute for eggs while baking. You can use 2 teaspoons of chia seeds and soak them in half a glass of water for a few minutes. They impart a unique velvety texture after getting soaked. They expand, become softer and render a gel-like texture to the mix, providing a refreshing dimension to your cooking.
- You can then use this water in making bread, muffins, and granola bars.

- You can also mix this water into the homemade fresh juices, smoothies or add them to porridges, puddings, and sauces.

Ingredients for green chia smoothie

- 2 cups of spinach
- 1–½ cups of water
- 2 tbsp of chia seeds

Method

i. Blend 2 cups of spinach with 1–½ cups of water and 2 tablespoons of chia seeds.
ii. Add 1 peeled orange, a cup of mixed berries of your choice and blend again. You can also try experimenting with melons instead of berries.
iii. Enjoy the drink!

3. Kadoo (pumpkin seeds)

Pumpkin seeds are derived from pumpkin fruit and are readily available in market at a relatively cheaper price as compared to other seeds. They contain an array of essential micronutrients ranging from magnesium, copper, iron and zinc. They are also rich in B vitamins, proteins and healthy fatty acids.

Essential features and benefits

- They are rich in amino acids, promoting muscle health and boosting metabolism.
- They carry densely packed copper, iron, magnesium and manganese.

- Containing cucurbitacins, an anti-inflammatory compound, they help in preventing prostate enlargement and diminishes the risk of the prostate as well as breast cancer.
- Including a decent amount of essential fatty acids, they help maintain healthy blood vessels, lowering LDL (bad) cholesterol level and increasing that of HDL (good) cholesterol in the blood.
- The anti-inflammatory properties of pumpkin seeds enable them to serve as a remedy for treating joint pain, thereby effective in combating arthritis.
- They contain bioactive compounds that can aid in preventing loss of hair.

INTERESTING FACTS

Stay calm and sleep well

Pumpkin seeds are rich in tryptophan, an amino acid that gets converted to serotonin by the nervous system. Serotonin assists in alleviating symptoms of anxiety and ensuring sound sleep at night.

Boost your prostate and bladder health

In naturopathy and herbal treatments, pumpkin seeds serve as an effective remedy to treat prostate disorders and urinary tract infections. Furthermore, they can help in controlling an overactive bladder.

Achieve your RDV of micronutrients

A couple of ounces of pumpkin seeds can entirely meet your daily requirement of copper, iron, manganese, phosphorus and magnesium. It implies that these seeds are extremely beneficial in promoting cardiac, bone, neural, neuronal and mental health, improving blood count and boosting cognitive functioning.

Consuming the vibrant seeds

- Eat them raw or dry roast them for a healthy snack. Roasting pumpkin seeds brings out their natural flavour.
- Sprinkle them over smoothies, Greek yogurt, fruit salads, soups or cereals.
- Use roasted pumpkin seeds as an ingredient in baking sweet or savoury bread and cakes.

4. Sunflower seeds

Sunflower is a modern-day plant that got commercialized as an oilseed crop as recently as in the mid-twentieth century. There are some arguments against using sunflower oil in cooking. However, nobody can deny the health benefits that its raw seeds impart.

Essential features and benefits

- Rich in the amino acids, they help promote muscle health and boost metabolism
- One of the most prolific sources of B complex vitamins, they play a critical role in promoting a healthy nervous system and uplifting mental health.
- Decent source of phosphorus, magnesium, iron, potassium and protein, they promote bone health and regulate blood pressure.
- The extremely high content of magnesium allows sunflower seeds the ability to prevent the risk of osteoporosis and arthritis.
- Being an excellent source of Vitamin E, they serve as a robust antioxidant, boosting immunity, promoting neural health and enhancing skin health.

- They exhibit anti-inflammatory properties that have been proven to help combat symptoms of cold and cough.
- Replete with manganese, copper and selenium, they help boost energy levels, prevent anaemia, promote bone health, which further reduces the risk of bone abnormalities and osteoporosis.
- The seeds are considered excellent for the skin as they contain essential fatty acids like linolenic, oleic and palmitic acid, all of which enhance the skin tone and render smoothness to the skin tissues.
- The seeds carry phytosterols, which potentially lower down your cholesterol levels, boost immunity and offer protection against certain types of cancers.

Note: Consume sunflower seeds in moderation because the plants tend to take up cadmium from soil. Eating its seeds regularly can elevate the levels of cadmium in the blood, inducing heavy metal toxicity. However, limiting the intake to two to three times a week should not be a worry.

Roast them for crunchy delight

- High in protein and low in carbs, sunflower seeds make for an ideal snack.
- Add them with your tempering herbs and spices while making stew or gravy of traditional vegetables and lentil dishes.
- Roast them for a crunchy delight and add them to your vegetable salad or rice dishes.

5. Sesame seeds

Sesame seeds are tiny and oval-shaped seeds imparting a

nutty flavour and mild crunch. In the Eastern part of the world, particularly in Hindu mythology, these delicate seeds are regarded highly as a blessing and symbol of immortality.

Essential features and benefits

- Sesame seeds are densely packed with iron and zinc, promoting cognitive health and improving blood count.
- They are rich in protein, calcium, phosphorus and magnesium, promoting muscle and bone health, ensuring proper DNA repair and improving insulin metabolism.
- They contain sesamin and sesamolin, which can help in lowering cholesterol levels.
- Excellent source of Vitamin E plus omega-6, they help enhance neural health and boost immunity.
- They help in adding elasticity to skin tissues, improving skin health.
- They aid in digestion and facilitate proper blood circulation.

Add nutty flavour of sesame seeds in your meals

- Eat them raw or dry roast them for a healthy snack. Chew them well to reap maximum benefits out of them.
- Garnish your smoothies, Greek yogurt, fruit salads, soups and cereals by sprinkling sesame seeds over them.
- Give a treat to yourself by preparing tahini (a Middle Eastern condiment) from ground sesame seeds. You can then spread the creamy tahini dip on toasts, mix it into pureed chickpeas, add it as hummus or use it as a sauce with dry vegetables.

Ingredients for tahini

- 1 cup of sesame seeds
- 4–5 teaspoons of olive oil
- 100 ml of water
- 4–5 crushed garlic cloves
- ½ lemon
- Salt to taste
- 2 teaspoons of sesame oil

Method

i.   Roast a cupful of sesame seeds till they are golden brown for optimal flavour. Cool them and add them in a blender and grind them to a fine powder.

ii. Add 4–5 teaspoons of olive oil to the powder to achieve desired consistency and blend well. Your tahini paste is ready.

iii. Pour the tahini paste into a bowl and add lemon juice from half a lemon, 4–5 crushed (not minced) garlic cloves, and salt to taste.

iv. Whisk the mixture vigorously to evolve into a thick homogenized mixture.

v.   As the mixture is well blended, add 100 ml water and 2 teaspoons of sesame oil and whisk it further until it gives a smooth texture of a cream.

vi. Pour in more water, lemon juice or salt, if needed, to achieve desired taste and consistency.

6. Melons seeds (of muskmelon and watermelon)

As refreshing and hydrating melons are in summers, their seeds can play a vital role for a healthy mind, heart and brain.

Essential features and benefits

- They are loaded with essential amino acids, boosting insulin metabolism, improving insulin sensitivity and helping control blood sugar levels.
- Melon seeds are rich in tryptophan, serving as a magical remedy for insomnia. Tryptophan is an amino acid that gets converted to serotonin by the nervous system. Serotonin assists in alleviating symptoms of anxiety and having a sound sleep at night.
- A prolific source of iron and various types of B vitamins, they enhance immunity, promote cognitive health and serve as memory boosters.
- The high fibre content aids in cleansing the gut, eliminating worms from the GI tract and supporting and maintaining weight loss.
- They are excellent source of omega-3 and omega-6 fatty acids, promoting cardiac health.
- A tea made from watermelon seeds serves as a natural diuretic and can be used for kidney cleansing.
- Enriched with vitamins A, C and E, they help in boosting immunity, improving vision health and promoting neural health.
- They serve as an excellent source of magnesium and phosphorus, building up the bone strength.
- Carrying antioxidants, they help in maintaining natural skin tone and glow and slow down the aging process of skin. This in turn promotes softer, younger-looking and healthier skin.
- They contain a potent antioxidant in the form of lycopene that can give enhance male fertility.
- The seeds can play a critical and pivotal role in regulating

blood pressure and preventing coronary heart diseases.
- Replete with amino acids and proteins, they help strengthen the hair follicles. Furthermore, the essential fatty acids carried by melon seeds go a long way in preventing hair damage.

Embrace the melon seeds

- Do not throw away muskmelon seeds while consuming the fruit. Separate the seeds from the fruit. Wash them and let them dry in the sun. Then, enjoy munching on them in your own good time.
- Make a tea of watermelon seeds by boiling a few of them in water and relishing the benefits.
- Roast the seeds for a crunchy delight each time you feel peckish and want to snack. If you desire, you can add a little olive oil, salt, lime juice and black pepper to the seeds while roasting.
- Add raw or roasted melon seeds to your fruit servings, veggie salads, yogurt and smoothies.
- Mix these seeds in your soups, stews and gravies to feel satiated and keep your hunger pangs away for extended periods.
- Take a teaspoon of dried and ground melon seeds and mix them well with 1 teaspoon of honey. Consume the mixture with a cup of lukewarm water twice a day to treat edema.

POPPY SEEDS ALSO SEND THEIR REGARDS

Poppy seeds, also known as khus khus, are the nutty oilseeds that have been an integral part of the Indian cuisine. These are primarily used to impart a soft and gooey texture to desserts and gravies of vegetables.

Treat yourself with mouth-savouring khus khus halwa

Roast poppy seeds in the ghee until golden brown. Pour in some milk and add whole ground cardamom and cook till the moisture dries up. Add jaggery powder and sauté some more. You can garnish it with almonds and raisins.

Benefits

Do not underestimate the tiny delicate grains, as they also offer an array of health benefits in treating a host of ailments.

- One of the most potent ingredients in enhancing male fertility
- Alleviates the symptoms of stress and improves sleep quality, treating insomnia
- Improves cognitive functioning, reducing the risk of dementia and Alzheimer's
- Keeps a check on LDL cholesterol, enhancing cardiac health
- Promotes digestive health

CONCLUSION

This is not the end but the beginning of changing your dietary habits. And the first step is to go natural.

Our ancestors consumed grains, fruits and vegetables which did not undergo any kind of artificial treatment. They had better life expectancy rate, with lesser prevalence of chronic diseases like diabetes, obesity and cancer. In fact, a significant number of chronic ailments related to impairment in metabolism have developed only over the last century.

Ironically, our deteriorating health and surge in epidemics began with the industrial revolution that, along with many other things, brought changes in our eating habits. So, it's logical to say that the progression of these ailments can be stopped and reversed only if we change our diet.

Always remember, 'Health is 80 per cent diet and 20 per cent genetic predisposition and exercise.'[56]

With so much awareness and scientific evidence, it's high time that we search more for healthier options while going walking past the food section of the supermarkets. I am reiterating here that it's all about making a habit.

However, having said a lot about healthier options in the form of ingredients and foods described in the book, I want to clearly state that the homemade foods that we eat

---

[56]'80 nutrition 20 exercise- What does it REALLY mean?', *STAYFIT&YUNG*, https://stayfitandyung.com/2016/05/80-nutrition-20-exercise/. Accessed on 21 December 2021.

daily are healthy as well, and in fact, way better than fast foods and packaged stuff.

The whole point of the book is to focus on much healthier options that we often overlook turning to the same old dishes with potatoes and rice, or buying packed products. It is our inherent cravings for flavoursome food with a lot of crunch, zest and spice and the lack of time that compel us to make adverse choices.

First and foremost, you must change your cooking oil, which is why I described the benefits of healthy oils that are loaded with essential fatty acids. By removing refined oils and packed stuff from your kitchen, you are eliminating 95 per cent of the sources through which artificial trans fats can enter your body.

And secondly, you need to start taking time out to prepare your food and stop ordering from restaurants as an easy way out. It is because you are inadvertently causing inflammation in the body, which is the root cause of all the cardiometabolic conditions.

It's also important to mention that I did not include any animal-based food in the book because they are one of the primary sources through which heavy metals can enter our bodies, causing toxicity and severe health conditions. Through the course of the book, you would have understood how healthy our fruits and veggies are, and how nuts, seeds, herbs and spices are densely packed with micronutrients. There has been a lot of hue and cry regarding the environmental damage that the animal food industry causes. But that's a debate for another time.

Currently, we are influenced by the visibility and accessibility of what is being sold and supplied to us. And unfortunately, these products are artificially processed food and eventually detrimental to our health. Therefore, we need to cultivate the habit of eating organic and wholesome food. And hence, we need to

- Have more fruits and vegetables for salads in our fridge than boxes of industrially processed fruit juices
- Snack on almonds, flaxseeds and other nuts and seeds instead of binging on packets of chips and cookies. Add a variety of spices and herbs to our cooking to add natural, zesty and enticing flavours to our food rather than running after instant-noodles for some artificial taste

As a famous quote, often ascribed to Hippocrates states, 'Let thy food be thy medicine...'[57], I hope that you start making these changes bit by bit.

Happy Eating!

---

[57]G. Wegener, "'Let Food Be Thy Medicine, And Medicine Be Thy Food": Hippocrates Revisited'. *Acta Neuropsychiatrica*, *26*(1), 2014, p: 1–3.

ACKNOWLEDGEMENTS

This book marks a significant phase of my life and I would like to take a moment to thank those who helped me work on it.

I am thankful to the publisher, Mr Kapish Mehra, for believing in me and offering incessant support while I wrote the book. It was incredible to see how he stuck by my side during the delays caused by the pandemic. I express my gratitude to the editor, Sakschi Verma, for helping me refine my work to make it more impactful. I would like to thank Amrita Chakravorty for designing such an aesthetically beautiful cover page.

I would like to acknowledge Mr Sanjay Sachdeva and Dr Alok Chopra who introduced me to the whole world of functional and integrative medicine. I cannot thank them enough for providing me the tools and guidance to walk on the path of futuristic medicine. Offering joined consultations to patients with Dr Chopra was an unforgettable experience and a tremendous learning curve for me.

I would also like to acknowledge and dedicate this book to my patients who have conquered their diseases by sheer grit and discipline and choosing a healthier lifestyle.